1 The A
2 Barbizon Hotel
3 The Belaire
4 Central Park Place
5 Citylights
6 The Columbia
7 The Copley
8 The Cosmopolitan
9 Crowne Plaza Hotel
10 Delmonico Plaza
11 515 Park Avenue
12 Four Seasons
13 The Gotham
14 Hotel Delmonico
15 Hotel Navarro
16 Hudson Tower
17 Hudson View East
18 Hudson View West
19 Mayfair House
20 McAlpin Hotel
21 Park Avenue Court
22 Park Belvedere
23 Princeton House
24 Rihga Royal
25 Statler Hilton
26 The Vanderbilt
27 Worldwide Plaza
28 Zeckendorf Towers

Developing

My Life

Developing

My Life

William Zeckendorf Jr.

with Joan Duncan Oliver

ORO
EDITIONS

To my wife, Nancy
my sister, Susie
my sons, William and Arthur
and my grandchildren, Jennifer and Arthur III

This is a book about a great gent
Who deals in mortar and wet cement.
In his sixtieth year,
We'd like to make clear,
He builds to sell and not to rent.

Adapted from a poem by
NANCY ZECKENDORF AND PHYLLIS WAGNER
written for Bill Zeckendorf's sixtieth birthday party
at Le Cirque

ORO EDITIONS

Publishers of Architecture, Art, and Design
Gordon Goff: Publisher
www.oroeditions.com
info@oroeditions.com

Published by ORO Editions

ORO Project Coordinator: Kirby Anderson
10 9 8 7 6 5 4 3 2 1 Second Edition

First published by Andrea Monfried Editions, LLC, New York in 2016

Library of Congress data available upon request. World Rights: Available

ISBN: 978-1-954081-33-8

Color Separations and Printing: ORO Group Ltd.
Printed in China.

International Distribution: www.oroeditions.com/distribution

FOREWORD

My father, William Zeckendorf Jr., established his own real estate business in New York in 1972, and by 1994 he had moved on to retirement in Santa Fe, New Mexico. By most business standards this is a relatively short career. But few individuals have achieved more or changed more neighborhoods than my father did in that brief time. *Developing: My Life* chronicles those years. It is the story of a driven man who accomplished much. Sadly, my father passed away just as he finished writing the book. But his widow, Nancy Zeckendorf, has carried out his vision, guiding his memoir into print.

With the name Zeckendorf, it was inevitable that my father would go into real estate. By the time he joined his father's company, Webb & Knapp, in 1953, my grandfather, William Zeckendorf Sr., was among the most famous developers in America. My father eventually became president of Webb & Knapp and played a significant role in such high-profile projects as Kips Bay Plaza, Park West Village, and Lincoln Towers in New York, as well as Century City in Los Angeles and Place Ville Marie in Montreal.

After going out on his own in the early 1970s, my father acquired and renovated half a dozen hotels, then went on to build more than a dozen major condominiums, including the Columbia, Park Belvedere, Copley, Belaire, and Zeckendorf Towers in Manhattan and Citylights in Queens. For commercial projects, he built Delmonico Plaza and the mixed-use development Worldwide Plaza. Spread over four prime acres in Midtown Manhattan, Worldwide Plaza was the subject of a four-part PBS series, *Skyscraper*, that gave viewers an unprecedented inside look at the complex world of real estate development. My father also developed the Rihga Royal, Crowne Plaza, and Four Seasons Hotels. Periodically, Nancy would take him to New Mexico to relax, but he needed another outlet for his energies and developed five major projects in Santa Fe in his spare time.

There are a number of successful real estate dynasties in New York. However, what differentiates our family is that all three generations of us are self-made. That was certainly true for my father. By 1971, my grandfather's business had collapsed, and my father had to start over with no company and no capital. One of the most important pieces of advice he ever gave me was: "To succeed in this business you can never look back."

In those early summers when I worked for him, he was building a hotel portfolio that included the Delmonico, Mayfair House, and Statler Hilton. He paid close attention to back-of-the-house operations and occupancy rates and did spectacularly well renovating hotel properties, improving operations, and then selling them at a large profit.

But when we spent time together on weekends or at night over a bottle of wine, he often said that what he really wanted to do was develop. Renovating and selling hotels was profitable but ultimately unsatisfying for him. The creative part of the business was development, and that's where he was headed.

By the time I returned from business school in 1984, my father's company had grown dramatically. He was now in full swing, and one project had turned into five, all going on at the same time. Over the next eighteen years he completed more than twenty buildings in Manhattan and Queens. In the process, he transformed neighborhoods from Union Square to Hell's Kitchen, from the Upper West Side to Long Island City. Few developers have done more to revitalize neglected parts of New York than he did during those years.

My father would chase a deal, secure financing, and then pore over floor plans with the architect. But as soon as the first shovel hit the ground, he moved on to the next deal. My brother, Arthur, and I, or one of the other project managers on his ever-growing staff, would take it from there, overseeing construction and directing sales and marketing.

I spent a tremendous amount of time with my father in those years, looking for investors halfway around the world. Some of my fondest memories are the many trips we made to Japan for the increasing amounts of capital his ever-expanding business demanded. On one trip a massive earthquake knocked us both to the floor of the Imperial Hotel. On the next trip, a major typhoon hit. Wisely, our hosts stopped inviting us to Tokyo and came to visit us in New York from then on.

On another occasion we were desperate for a construction loan for Worldwide Plaza and had pinned our hopes on a major Canadian bank. On the day a senior bank officer whom we'd never met was scheduled to come to our office, we happened to have been invited to a lunch cruise aboard a friend's yacht. We took the banker with us on the cruise, where he seemed to be especially fond of the bar and buffet.

After the cruise, we were almost back at our office before we realized we had forgotten the banker and left him stranded aboard the yacht. We were sure we'd blown our chances of getting any financing. But to our amazement, a week later a loan commitment letter arrived from the Canadian bank.

As my father's creativity fueled his ambitions, all he wanted to do was build more and more. Money had never been of much interest to him, so it probably should not have been a surprise that when the recession hit the real estate market in 1991, he was undercapitalized. It was tough going for all of us, but my father handled this difficult time with amazing dignity, doing everything in his power to honor his obligations. By 1994, however, my father was ready to step back from real estate in New York, and soon thereafter he moved to Santa Fe.

I am thankful for the years I worked with my father and grateful for the many lessons he passed on. I will forever cherish the time we spent together.

William Lie Zeckendorf
New York City, 2016

COLLABORATOR'S NOTE

I first met Bill Zeckendorf Jr. in his room at Mt. Sinai Hospital in New York, where he was being treated for chronic obstructive pulmonary disease. He was sitting by the window, which overlooked Central Park. Pointing toward the West Side skyline, he said, "A lot of the buildings over there are my father's or mine." Just how many buildings were theirs I was to find out in the months to come.

Bill's sister, Susan, had recruited me to help out with the book he was writing. I knew the name Zeckendorf: anyone who lived in New York in the 1970s and 1980s had seen it posted on construction sites all over town. I also knew something about the family from Susie, a longtime friend. Though retired as a literary agent she was determined to help Bill publish his memoir, so she placed her memories—and family photos—at my disposal.

Bill and I started exchanging emails and phone calls. He was a man of few words, but those few were well chosen. Once or twice a week, he would send me three or four paragraphs about one project or another, with a bit of backstory about the people involved and maybe a sentence or two about what was happening in the city at the time. Slowly, brick by brick, we began building his life story.

Then I was invited to spend a week in Santa Fe, where Bill and his wife, Nancy, were living. Bill's health was fragile, so I figured that at most we would spend three or four hours a day working on the book. How wrong I was. When I arrived every morning at 9:00, Bill had been up for hours, typing away on his computer and downloading material from the Internet. Seated side by side in capacious armchairs in what Bill called his "music room"—a nod to the sound system that dominated one wall—we would work through the morning, break for a working lunch, then resume until mid-afternoon. Friends or colleagues of Bill's came by to contribute their recollections, and our conversation continued most evenings over dinner. I have hours of recordings of Bill, his voice barely above a whisper, recounting story after story about his life and his work. I can still hear his voice in my head.

To collaborate on a memoir is an extraordinary privilege. My only regret is that neither Bill nor his sister Susie lived to hold the finished book in their hands. Bill died just as he wound up the last chapter, and it fell to Nancy to shepherd his memoir through the publishing process. A woman of enormous accomplishment in her own right, Nancy was Bill's development partner in the Santa Fe years and his confidante throughout their fifty-year marriage. It was a joy to work with her on bringing the book to light.

I dedicate my part in this endeavor to Bill, a singular man who led an extraordinary life, and to Nancy, who lived it alongside him. And also to Susie, who championed her brother's writing through the very last draft.

Joan Duncan Oliver
New York City, 2016

Introduction

Bill Zeckendorf during construction of Zeckendorf Towers, New York, with Con Edison building in the background (opposite)

I'll never forget that afternoon in March 1988. The phone rang: it was Tom Javits, my project manager at the Belaire, a forty-two-story apartment tower we were building on Manhattan's Upper East Side. "We've got a problem, Bill," Tom began. "A big one. You'd better get over here right away." Tom's not one to exaggerate, so I could tell it was bad.

The site was a ten-minute drive from our office, but my driver probably made it in half that time. When I got there, I saw Tom, the building engineer, and the excavation crew lined up along the rim of the hole, peering into it with worried looks. The excavation was nearly finished, but when the bulldozers had reached the outer edge of the site, the crew had discovered that the apartment building next door wasn't resting on a foundation, just on mud—and it was drifting our way. If we didn't do something fast we'd have eighteen stories of brick and glass tumbling into our site.

Skyscrapers in New York City need to be anchored to bedrock to prevent settling. They generally rest on a reinforced-concrete foundation that sits on the rock. However, the apartment tower due west of us, which went up in 1963, wasn't built to code. The mistake was theirs—an illegal shortcut that had eluded the building inspectors—but the problem was ours—under the city's building codes, shoring up *their* building was *our* responsibility. So we had to stop work and underpin the leaning tower, setting us back four months. All the while, the clock was ticking on our construction loan. Thousands of dollars in interest were mounting while we put in a new foundation for the building next door.

But eventually, we finished the Belaire, and it was one of our most successful projects. We received kudos for the innovative design, and the luxury condos sold well. But the excavation delay wasn't the last of our problems—not by a long shot. In the development business, that's just the way it goes.

Not every job encounters the problems we faced at the Belaire, but the unexpected is to be expected. Crises, problems, overruns, delays: they're all built into the cost of development. Putting up a building is never dull.

I learned that early on. I was born to the trade, after all. In his heyday, my father, William Zeckendorf Sr., was the most famous and successful developer in America—a larger-than-life presence who reshaped the skyline from one coast to the other. If you stand on the East Side of Manhattan and look west over Central Park, many of the buildings you see were built by my father. (You can see a few of mine there, too.) I started hanging around my father's office when I was just a boy. As the years went on, I was thrown into some of the most exciting projects of the postwar building boom, with some of the best architects of the twentieth century. I.M. Pei got his start as my father's in-house architect, and I still have the desk I.M. designed for Dad's office.

My father was such a force, with such an outsized personality, that people sometimes aren't aware that another Zeckendorf—his namesake at that—came along right behind him. But I put my own mark on the New York cityscape with pioneering projects that opened up marginal neighborhoods and overlooked sites. I was never the showman my father was, never had an in-house PR team at the ready, as he did. That's not my style. But at the height of my career in the 1980s, I was the busiest developer in New York, and I never lost the thrill.

People often ask me what a developer does. Every project is different, I tell them, but generally it involves assembling property for a building site; finding equity partners and arranging financing for land and construction; working with an architect on a design; hiring a contractor to supervise construction and oversee subcontractors and construction crews; marketing the offices or apartments, selling and leasing them to potential occupants—and dealing with any number of crises and setbacks along the way. When I explain this, the reaction often is, "Wow! Why would anybody want to go through all that?"

That's not a question I ever asked myself during more than fifty years in the business. Though some projects were more interesting than others, some were more profitable than others, and some brought more challenges or headaches than others, I never doubted my choice.

Why did I find real estate development so compelling? The answer is simple: *I wanted to build.*

Developing is clearly in my genes. Though my father's shoes were big ones to fill, I loved and admired him, and I learned a lot from him. His passion for development was infectious. With that and the name Zeckendorf, it was inevitable that I would end up on one side or another of the family business.

Still, people sometimes wonder, didn't I ever want to break out and do something different? I can honestly say no. Sure, after I dropped out of college I briefly considered becoming a Broadway producer: I loved working backstage when I was in school. But I always knew that my best opportunity lay in working for my father. By the time I entered my teens, I was spending summers and school vacations working for Dad. And from the moment I picked up my discharge papers from the army, I worked alongside him at his company, Webb & Knapp, until it folded in 1965.

After that, I went out on my own, forming what would become the Zeckendorf Company. Even then, my father remained a presence, advising me on properties and projects. And as soon as my sons, William Lie and Arthur William, were old enough, they came to work for me.

Over the past half century, I've renovated and built hotels, put up office towers and apartment buildings, and pioneered in emerging areas. I've earned a reputation as a visionary who could see potential where others couldn't, whether in an oddly shaped lot or a rundown block. With my projects, I turned around struggling neighborhoods, improving life for the residents and paving the way for future development.

Ask me which project I'm proudest of, and I would cite a few, all quite different. The Columbia condominium was my first building from the ground up; it opened the Upper West Side to residential development and set off a building boom all the way down the Broadway corridor from West 96th Street to Union Square. On Union Square, I built Zeckendorf Towers, named for my father. A mixed-use complex, it seeded the rebirth of a once blighted area, transforming it from a haven for drug dealers to the thriving hub it is today—home of the city's largest greenmarket and a bustling crossroads of downtown New York life.

Eighth Avenue between West 49th and 50th Streets is the site of one of my largest projects, Worldwide Plaza; the office building and condo tower fill an entire four-acre city block. To upgrade this neighborhood, the infamous Hell's Kitchen, we renovated rundown tenements, shut down drug dens, and razed sex shops and peep shows, making Midtown west of Broadway a viable location for blue-chip businesses and upscale residences.

And then there's the Four Seasons, a luxury hotel on East 57th Street. This project gave me a chance to work with I.M. Pei, not only my father's house architect for years but also a close Zeckendorf family friend. Assembling the site where the hotel

William Zeckendorf Sr. on one of his two car phones

stands—a patchwork of eleven properties—is a textbook case in how to put together a development deal.

With a team of investors and partners, I worked for more than a decade on a massive government project, the Ronald Reagan Building and International Trade Center in Washington, D.C. After the Pentagon, it's the largest office complex in the capital. I still remember the thrill of sitting on the dais with Nancy Reagan and President Bill Clinton for the dedication ceremony.

I have a special soft spot for Queens West, the development project that opened the Queens waterfront for residential use. There's a famous photograph of my father standing on a grassy knoll near the East River, with the United Nations Secretariat Building in the distance behind him. That spot is almost exactly where, decades later, we broke ground for Citylights, the first building in an urban renewal project that transformed an industrial wasteland into prime residential riverfront property. My dad assembled the land on which the UN was built, so whenever I see that photo, I feel proud of the part the Zeckendorfs played in international history.

Then there are the Santa Fe projects. I'm proud of these for many reasons, not least because my wife, Nancy, has been a guiding force behind them. A former principal ballerina for the Metropolitan Opera, she worked tirelessly for American Ballet Theatre and other cultural organizations while we were living

Bill Zeckendorf with a model of Worldwide Plaza

in New York and then went on to reshape the cultural landscape of Santa Fe, New Mexico, by transforming the landmark Lensic theater into a vibrant, twenty-first-century performing arts center.

For years, I put off writing about my life in development. I'm pretty private, and I'd rather do something than talk about it. I figured my work could speak for itself. But now that a fourth generation of Zeckendorfs is coming along—my granddaughter is in the class of 2016 at the Columbia Graduate School of Architecture, Planning and Preservation, and my grandson is in the class of 2015 at Columbia Business School—I feel a strong desire to set the record straight.

I'm my father's son, but I'm not my father. I forged my own path, did my own deals, and raised two extremely successful sons who have built a multibillion-dollar business in residential real estate. My own career did not follow a straight upward trajectory. I've experienced setbacks and losses. I'm not a gambler, but real estate development is inherently risky, and I happened to be in the game at the end of the 1980s, when the market went south and took my holdings with it.

The Zeckendorf name opened many doors, sometimes in unexpected and unusual ways. I'm eternally grateful for that. But it was no protection against the vagaries of real estate or some of my partners. My father soared high and then fell spectacularly, like Icarus. In helping him close up his business, I vowed not to follow in his footsteps. Instead, I made my own mistakes before ending on a high note, with a second, satisfying career in Santa Fe. Along the way I've worked with exceptional people—architects, contractors, investors, brokers, city planners, and a loyal and committed office staff. And through it all, Nancy has been beside me.

Developing: My Life is a legacy of sorts. I offer it to answer, at least in part: Who was Bill Zeckendorf Jr.? What did he build? And what did he discover along the way?

Educating the Master

Having a famous father is both a curse and a blessing. My father, William Zeckendorf Sr., was so widely known in his day that even with *Junior* appended to my name, I lived in his shadow. My earliest years were rocky, disrupted by my parents' divorce. But it wasn't long before my father swept me along as his business—and influence—reached world-class proportions. Everything I learned about real estate development came from observing him in action.

My father was creative, charismatic, and virtually unstoppable. His successes and failures were equally dramatic. Living and working by his side was a priceless education. For better and worse, growing up Zeckendorf made me the man I am.

Growing Up Zeckendorf

[Bill] learned quickly and accepted responsibility.
I gave him all the exposure I could; he was my companion
and advisor on all new developments.

WILLIAM ZECKENDORF SR., *Zeckendorf*

I was born in New York on October 31, 1929, a week after Black Thursday. Not an auspicious start: the whole country was in turmoil. My father, however, sailed through the crisis—at least to hear him tell it. It took a year or so after the stock market crash for the real estate market to tank. My father, who was just starting out as a broker, used the downturn to his advantage. As people were squeezed to sell off real estate, he worked both sides of the trend. With one hand, he helped owners renegotiate mortgages so they wouldn't lose their holdings; with the other, he was selling foreclosed properties.

Young Bill Zeckendorf (left)

Irma Zeckendorf (née Levy)

Bill with his sister, Susan

I was my parents' first child. At the time, my father and mother, the former Irma Levy, were living in a small apartment at Lexington Avenue and East 94th Street. After my sister, Susan, was born in 1931, we moved to 944 Park Avenue. The apartment took up an entire floor. "Under normal circumstances," my father wrote in his autobiography, *Zeckendorf*, "we could never have afforded such a place, but I was occupying it in return for help I had given to a friend." Even then he was spending more than he made. "By the standards of the 1930's," he said, "we were affluent—even if often broke."

Overextending himself was the eventual undoing of my father's extraordinary career. As a child, I was unaware of his rising and falling fortunes, but they would come to have an abiding effect on my own life and career.

My parents could not have been more different. Dad was gregarious and outgoing, a large, ebullient man who worked hard and liked a good time. My mother was more introverted, with tastes that were cultural and intellectual. Dad went along with her love of opera, theater, and dance up to a point, but by 1934 their diverging interests—and my father's wandering eye—were too apparent to ignore. They divorced when I was five.

Overnight, my life changed completely. My mother married the noted music critic Irving Kolodin and moved my sister and me to an apartment on Seventh Avenue near Carnegie Hall. A few years later, we moved again, to a bigger apartment in the St. Urban, an impressive Beaux-Arts building on Central Park West in the 80s. It was within walking distance of Collegiate, the private school I attended. When my stepfather went into the army in World War II, my mother moved us to an apartment on West 67th Street, across the street from the famed Hotel des Artistes. Our building was next door to a stable, and the stench was overwhelming. My father later bought the stable, then sold it to the American Broadcasting Company—a canny move. Although 67th Street was a haven for creative people, our apartment was so small that there was barely room to turn around. I vowed never to live like that again.

Bill at Lawrenceville

After the divorce, my father moved into the Hotel Lombardy on East 56th Street, where my grandparents kept an apartment on another floor. Weekends, my sister and I would take the bus across town to see Dad. I don't remember much about those early years. My mother and I had little in common, but I adored my father, though he was often preoccupied. Looking back, I see that the divorce cut deep in ways I never fully acknowledged.

When I was thirteen, I was sent to Lawrenceville, a boarding school near Princeton, New Jersey. My father had remarried by then, but during school vacations I stayed with him, downstairs in a small maid's room in the apartment building where he and my stepmother Marion lived.

My first year at Lawrenceville, I was miserable. A big, shy kid, I was one of only a few Jewish boys in the school, and I was uncomfortably aware of it. I hadn't run into anti-Semitism before that. My family were non-practicing Jews: I don't recall ever observing a Jewish holiday or attending services of any kind. But at one point, my mother decided that my sister and I should have some sort of religious education, so she hired a rabbi to come to our apartment and teach us about religion. A few of our friends were invited to join us: among them was Johnny Gunther, who died of a brain tumor at seventeen—a tragedy that his father, the journalist John Gunther, wrote about movingly in

Death Be Not Proud. I vaguely remember one or two classes with the rabbi, but the whole experiment was short-lived.

By the end of that first, unhappy year at Lawrenceville, I realized I had two options: I could be miserable for three more years, or I could get involved in student life. I chose the latter. I joined the drama society and spent long hours backstage on production. I signed on with the school newspaper and later with the yearbook staff. I became a big man on campus, running every organization I joined and earning a nickname: the Boss. Transforming myself from a lonely outsider to the Boss was a lesson in turning a bad situation to my advantage that would prove useful throughout my career.

However, I spent so much time running things that I didn't pay much attention to my studies. I managed to scrape through, but my grades were average—except in French, which I nearly flunked. Senior year, I decided I didn't want to go to college, so I didn't bother applying. Then the summer after graduation I went to Europe with a cousin and a friend who were entering Yale that fall. Suddenly, I wanted to go to Yale. I applied at the last minute, and to no one's surprise I was turned down. I've regretted not going to Yale ever since. Friendships formed there would have benefitted my career, I'm sure.

As usual, my father had the answer. He picked up the phone and called his cousin Harold Steinfeld in Tucson, Arizona. Harold, who owned Steinfeld's, Tucson's leading department store, happened to be chairman of the board of the University of Arizona. This time, to no one's surprise I was accepted. I started classes in the fall of 1948.

After a small Eastern prep school, the University of Arizona was overwhelming. It was huge, and I knew no one. Harold Steinfeld and his wife, Peggy, became my safe haven. They lived in a penthouse on top of the Pioneer Hotel, which Harold owned. Years later, they died tragically when the hotel burned to the ground.

The Zeckendorfs and Steinfelds were pioneers, among the wave of German Jewish immigrants who settled in the Southwest in the mid-nineteenth century. They went first to New Mexico and then to Arizona. I knew none of this family history while I was at the University of Arizona. I only found out about my heritage many years later when I developed my first project in Santa Fe.

Nice as the Steinfelds were, they couldn't keep me in Tucson. The classes bored me, and I wanted to work, so I left college in my sophomore year. I was following in my father's footsteps: he had dropped out of New York University.

I worked in summer stock in Atlantic City at one point, so after Tucson I briefly considered becoming a Broadway producer, but that notion was short-lived. It was obvious I would be better off working for Dad. For my first assignment, he sent me to St. Louis, Missouri, to assist the project manager on a five-hundred-unit apartment building that was under construction. The project manager wasn't doing a very good job, however, so my father fired him. He was a retired colonel, and after he was let go, he was appointed head of the draft board in New York.

Bill and army buddies in Korea

The Korean War had started by then, and I had lost my deferment by dropping out of college. To keep from being drafted, I had joined the local unit of the Army Reserves in St. Louis. (It happened to be an intelligence unit.) Even so, one day the colonel called my father and said, "I'm going to have your son arrested for dodging the draft." Clearly, I wasn't dodging the draft, but he scared the hell out of me, and rather than put up a fight, I signed up for active duty.

I was sent overseas as an infantryman. When I got to Korea, the brass were looking for someone for the G-2—the intelligence section. When they saw my record they assigned me to Command Headquarters in Pusan, on the southeastern tip of the Korean peninsula, five hundred miles behind the front lines.

I was given the job of collecting telexes from all the divisions and writing up overnight activities in the war zone for the 5:00 AM briefing of the General Staff. My supervisor, a colonel, would deliver the report while I stood beside him pointing out battle positions on a map. But my real job came after the briefing. The colonel would call me into his office and hang a sign outside his door that read, "Top secret meeting. Do not disturb." Then the two of us would play chess until lunchtime. I had learned to play chess at Lawrenceville, and though I wasn't very good, I was better than anyone else around. Eventually I started beating the colonel, but I was careful not to win too often.

At one of the briefings, we were told that our group had been selected to handle the first exchange of wounded prisoners—American, Korean, and Chinese. I went to the colonel in charge of the exchange and asked to join his team.

Called Operation Little Switch, the exchange took place at Panmunjom, up north on the 38th parallel near the demilitarized zone. My job was to check off the names of the soldiers being released by North Korea. Our wounded had been poorly cared for, and they looked half-starved, but it was wonderful to see them coming out alive. I had my camera with me and took pictures until the North Koreans and Chinese objected. They didn't want us to photograph their wounded. Later, I was assigned to the final prisoner exchange, Operation Big Switch.

When I got back to headquarters after the first prisoner exchange, someone had taken my place at the briefings. There was also a different colonel in charge, and he was annoyed that I'd taken off, so he sent me to Incheon, back up north. I exchanged the comforts of headquarters for a cot in a tent in the snow. The only time I came close to seeing action during my entire tour was when a North Korean in a tiny plane tried to bomb our petrol tanks. He missed, and my contribution was to retrieve the bomb fragments and send them to headquarters for analysis.

One day while I was still in Pusan, I got a call from the office of Syngman Rhee, the president of South Korea. Could I come for tea with President Rhee and his wife? That was like being asked to tea at the White House—only in this case the president's house was blue. I was just an enlisted man, a corporal. I couldn't figure out why I was being asked, but I knew I would be debriefed after the visit, so I took along another soldier from the intelligence section as a witness.

President Rhee and his Austrian wife were surprisingly gracious, considering my low rank. We talked a little about how the war was going, and Rhee said how grateful he was for the Americans' help. Just chitchat, but I found out why I had been invited to tea with South Korea's leader. It seems that my father had been seated next to the Korean ambassador at a United Nations dinner and had mentioned he was worried because he hadn't heard from me.

Toward the end of the war, a group known as the American-Korean Foundation was formed in New York to help in the reconstruction of South Korea. The board members included Dr. Howard Rusk of the Rusk Institute of Rehabilitation Medicine and Lieutenant General James A. Van Fleet, former commander of the American forces in Korea. My father made sure I was included when the group toured the ravished country. It was quite an experience. My only complaint was that I got a sore arm from saluting all the brass.

I was discharged from the army near the end of 1953 and went back to work for my father. He assigned me to another troubled project, this time an apartment complex built alongside a shopping center in San Diego. The idea was that prospective buyers would be attracted by the convenience and, once they bought, would patronize the mall. In principle, it should have worked, but in fact, nothing was selling. The 500 or so apartments in the complex were 100 percent empty.

Dad put me in touch with the publisher of San Diego's newspapers, who referred me to a retired naval officer who knew his way around the nearby base. San Diego is a big navy town, the home port of the Pacific Fleet. The officer suggested that instead of trying to sell the apartments, we should offer them as short-term rentals. I figured that servicemen returning from Korea would be a ready market, provided the apartments were furnished. The strategy worked. After we furnished the apartments and advertised them, they filled up right away. The apartment complex consisted of rambling, two-story wooden buildings that were little more than barracks. Dad had never intended it to be a long-term investment, and with tenants in place, we were able to sell it.

Learning the Business

Bill saw opportunity. He was a dealmaker. And he was an extremely hard worker. I think that's what he got from working for his father. He was in the trenches every day.

DAVID CHILDS, partner, Skidmore, Owings & Merrill

That my father could orchestrate a meeting with the president of Korea or the most influential man in San Diego wasn't a surprise. By the mid-1950s he had established himself as the most famous developer in the country, maybe even the world.

Dad's reputation had reached global proportions a decade earlier, when he provided the land for the UN Secretariat. He had assembled seventeen acres along Manhattan's East River—most of it filled with slaughterhouses and cattle pens—for "X City," a monumental, futuristic complex he envisioned building on a platform over the river. But it was a mad plan, and when Dad heard that New York was about to lose the United

X-City project, New York, 1946 (left)

East River site in New York (current home of United Nations) assembled by William Zeckendorf Sr.

Nations to Philadelphia, he offered to sell his land to the organization for its headquarters. The UN couldn't come up with the cash, so John D. Rockefeller Jr. bought the land for $8.5 million and donated it to the UN. The contract was signed at Fefe's Monte Carlo nightclub, which Webb & Knapp owned. For many years I kept above my desk a copy of Rockefeller's check, made out to my father, along with a copy of the contract of sale.

As Dad was buying up the land along the East River, one parcel eluded him, the block between 48th and 49th Streets. Twenty years later, in one of the last deals I did for my father, and one of the most complicated, I was able to put together the financing to buy it. Now twin apartment towers, 860 and 870 United Nations Plaza, occupy the site.

In 1956, the United Nations played another role in my life: Guri Lie—my first wife and the mother of my sons, Will and Arthur—was the daughter of Trygve Lie, the first UN secretary-general.

My father was a true visionary, renowned for his bold imagination and outsized ambitions. He loved nothing more than a challenge, the more impossible the better. His motto, he once told a reporter, was "You can never tell till you try." I knew I couldn't match his imagination or brilliance, but I like to think that some of his passion for developing rubbed off on me. Not that I was an "uninhibited opportunist," as Dad once described himself—unless you think of opportunism as being able to spot a property with promise, and then doing whatever it takes to maximize its potential.

Dad never sat me down and said, "Someday, son, this will all be yours." But ironically, in 1956, at the height of his career, the *New Yorker* ran a cartoon of a father gesturing to the New York City skyline as he tells the child at his side, "Someday, my boy, all this will belong to Mr. William Zeckendorf." I suppose my father just assumed I would follow in his footsteps. I spent summer vacations working for him from the time I was ten or eleven. Initially, I was a clerk and messenger. My father was still a broker then, and my first assignment was to deliver some legal papers to a woman whose property he had just sold. When I was sixteen, I set foot on a construction site for the first time. The building was at 1407 Broadway, near West 38th Street. Every

Whitney Darrow Jr., cartoon from the *New Yorker*, March 31, 1956

"Someday, my boy, all this will belong to Mr. William Zeckendorf."

Friday, I would take the construction elevator up the outside of the building and deliver paychecks to the ironworkers on the high girders. Riding the rickety open-sided hoist to the windy upper floors was terrifying, and I wouldn't go near the steel girders. I'm afraid of heights and have avoided construction elevators ever since. But at the time I was willing to endure a little fear for the chance to watch a skyscraper go up.

My father and I were close, though our personalities were miles apart. I was a listener, my father a talker. I was soft-spoken, he was a shouter. He made friends instantly, I took longer. He plunged into deals, I mulled things over. He aspired to remake entire cities, I was content to improve neighborhoods.

We worked together successfully for twelve years. The projects were my father's, though as the business grew, so did my responsibilities. Soon Dad was relying on me to round up financing to save a project or bail him out of a tight spot. Eventually, I was named president of his company, Webb & Knapp. But there was never any doubt who was in charge.

The first test of my rainmaking talent was at Place Ville Marie in Montreal. This was my father's grand plan for developing the former Canadian National Railway yards as an office complex built around a plaza and underground shops. I was the construction manager—no small challenge since we had to work around anti-American sentiment in Canada at the time, along with opposition from Montreal's conservative banking and business elite. Not to mention construction glitches and underfunding.

In late 1958, construction nearly ground to a halt when we ran out of money. The engineers informed me that there wasn't enough steel in the building to keep it from swaying dangerously in high winds—we would have to add more. By the time we finished negotiating with the steel companies, we not only had to pay for new steel but also had to pony up additional money for the steel that had already gone up. After my father failed in his efforts to bring in more funds, I flew to London to see Jack Cotton, a friend of my father's who was England's most prominent developer at the time. Cotton had made a verbal commitment for $25 million, and I assumed I was going to London to close the deal. At our first meeting, however, Cotton suggested we meet again two days later. In the meantime, I had a get-acquainted lunch with Kenneth Keith of the London investment bank Philip Hill, Higginson, Erlanger's (later Hill Samuel). Keith was a venture financier I thought I might want to do business with in the future. I told him about Place Ville Marie and my deal with Cotton.

Good thing I did. Before our second meeting, Cotton called me with bad news. He had just built the Pan Am Building in New York, and the Bank of England wouldn't let him take any more money out of the country. Those were the banking regulations at the time, but I could tell that Cotton had also gotten cold feet. Perhaps he had second thoughts about the risk of doing business with my father or about the project itself. Whatever his reason, the money we desperately needed had evaporated.

I was distraught. Without Cotton, we would have to stop construction. I went back to Philip Hill and told them what had happened. We worked out a deal for the $25 million we needed.

Unfortunately, that wasn't the end of our problems, so not long after, I flew back to London, going straight to the bank. I knew it was risky to ask for more money when we hadn't even received the first $25 million we'd agreed on. But Philip Hill told me they wanted to invest $10 million in Webb & Knapp. That

Queen Elizabeth II and William Zeckendorf Sr. with a model of Place Ville Marie, Montreal

infusion enabled us to finish Place Ville Marie, which turned out to be one of my father's best projects.

With the financing for Place Ville Marie locked in, J. P. Morgan, one of our bankers, hosted a dinner in New York to celebrate. Ever the showman, my father chose that moment to announce that he'd dropped $1 million of Philip Hill's $10 million on a new private plane. That was all our new British investment partner had to hear. Well aware of my father's increasingly risky leveraging, as well as the risk his own bank was taking on, the Philip Hill banker shouted at Dad, "We didn't invest in your company in order to buy a new airplane! And you didn't even ask our permission!" No punches were thrown, but the two men fought at the top of their lungs. Finally, the chairman of J. P. Morgan intervened and tried to broker an understanding; he even suggested we hire someone my father would have to report to before making any purchases. But you couldn't curb my father. If he wanted to do something, he'd do it.

After that evening, the relationship with Philip Hill went sour. It was a harbinger of things to come. Business for Dad, and for Webb & Knapp, would never be the same. But we still had a few good years left.

My father was a fantastic salesman, and there was never a dull moment as he pulled off some of his "impossible" deals. Once when we were in Los Angeles together, the movie mogul Spyros Skouras invited us to tour 20th Century Fox. We were astounded to see 263 acres of prime real estate adjoining Beverly Hills devoted to a movie studio and its back lot. Dad told Spyros he wanted to buy the land. Spyros said he would never sell.

Things change fast in real estate, however. And at the time, the studio system was changing, too: 20th Century Fox, like other movie companies, was looking for ways to raise cash. When the cost of making the film *Cleopatra* nearly bankrupted Fox, Spyros put the land on the market. He called Dad to see if he still wanted to buy it. My father said no, that it was overpriced. Then he managed to talk the price down and finagle a deal by which Webb & Knapp would buy the land in parcels

Century City, Los Angeles

over a ten-year period while leasing the studio back to Fox. It was a brilliant plan.

Dad needed backing, however, so he turned to the Aluminum Company of America (now Alcoa). I was with Dad when he went to see Alcoa in Pittsburgh. We met with the top executives, and my father tried to excite them with his dream of an aluminum city. The executives listened politely, then excused themselves to discuss the matter. We returned to their office after lunch, and for two hours listened to them explain all the reasons not to back us. Then there was a pause. We were getting ready to leave when they said, "Okay, when do you need the money?" They were unlikely partners, but Dad convinced Alcoa that aluminum-sheathed buildings would be a great way to showcase their product.

A few years before he sold the land, Spyros had asked Welton Becket, a West Coast architect, to devise a master plan for developing it. After we bought the property, I worked closely with Becket on plans for what we would call Century City. The first year we put a road in, but the rest of the tract was so barren that Alcoa said we ought to plant wildflowers on it. So there we were, out in the field tossing seeds around.

Becket's vision for Century City was a "city within a city," with office and residential high-rises, a hotel, a shopping center,

President Dwight D. Eisenhower, William Zeckendorf Sr., center, and Bill Zeckendorf, second from right, with rendering of L'Enfant Plaza, Washington, D.C.

parks, and landscaped plazas, all carefully sited with plenty of open space and an "avenue of the stars," modeled on the Champs-Élysées in Paris, running through it. Becket brought in world-class architects like Minoru Yamasaki, I.M. Pei, and Skidmore, Owings & Merrill to design buildings. The first building in the complex was Gateway West, an office tower completed in 1963 that was one of several Becket designed.

Century City was Alcoa's first venture into real estate but far from the last. The deal was profitable for them and got Webb & Knapp out of hot water. And the complex is still cited as one of the most successful urban redevelopment projects in America.

Redeveloping ill-used or undervalued land to the benefit of the community was a specialty of my father's. Working with him on Society Hill Towers—the restoration of a historic section of Philadelphia—and L'Enfant Plaza in southwest Washington, D.C., set the stage for my own interest in undervalued properties and my commitment to projects that improved neighborhoods and enhanced the well-being of the residents.

In New York, I worked with my father on Kips Bay Plaza, built in 1962 as middle-income rental housing under Title I of the 1949 Housing Act. (The complex has since been converted into highly desirable market-rate condos.) Consisting of twin towers and a private garden covering several city blocks in the East 30s, Kips Bay Plaza was an innovative design by I.M. Pei. My father was always a great supporter of good architecture: he felt strongly that it was the obligation of developers to strive for good design. I took that to heart when I started to build. The Kips Bay towers are beautiful, with window walls offering city and river views—unheard of in middle-income housing at the time. Also unusual was the construction material: while most residential buildings at the time were brick, at Kips Bay they're poured concrete. Both Pei and my father were such perfectionists that we ended up buying a cement plant in New Jersey to get the mix just right.

Another urban redevelopment project I worked on with my father was Park West Village in Manhattan Valley on the Upper West Side. This, too, was Title I housing and another partnership between Webb & Knapp and Alcoa. Consisting of four red-brick towers designed by Skidmore, Owings & Merrill, Park West Village replaced blocks of tenements with airy apartments in a parklike setting. Like Kips Bay Plaza, Park West Village has since been converted to market-rate condos.

Kips Bay Plaza, New York, after completion of the first residential building (left)

Site plan for Kips Bay Plaza showing the two buildings

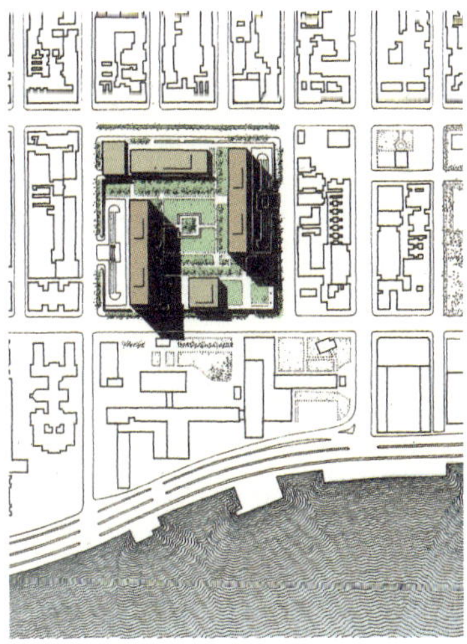

Park West Village is just blocks from my first development site at Broadway and West 96th Street. The Columbia condominium wasn't a Title I project, but it was urban renewal of sorts. The high-rise turned a once marginal neighborhood into a haven for young families and first-time apartment owners, and launched a run of residential development down the Broadway corridor.

Tagging along with my father as he scouted properties and made deals led to meeting some interesting people. Howard Hughes, for one. Spyros Skouras called my father to say that the famously eccentric Hughes wanted to sell his businesses and devote his resources to medical research. My father thought the Rockefellers might be interested, so Laurance Rockefeller, Dad, and I flew to Los Angeles to meet with Hughes. Hughes was obsessive-compulsive and paranoid, and the visit turned into a cloak-and-dagger adventure worthy of the big-budget action films he was producing at the time.

There was much getting in and out of different cars before we were finally told the meeting was off. Hughes had said he would meet with only two people, and I made three. Once Dad sent me back to the hotel, the meeting was back on. Later, when they were about to fly to Las Vegas to inspect Hughes's properties, Hughes relented and said I could come along. We had to fly in and out of the Las Vegas airport, and enter and leave our hotel, under cover of darkness, accompanied by more getting in and out of cars. It was like a French farce. And in the end, it was all for nothing. Hughes wasn't ready to sell. He was stringing us along, my father said—probably just fishing to see what his properties were worth.

Another living legend I encountered with Dad was the architect Frank Lloyd Wright. My father met him while we were in Chicago working on the redevelopment of Hyde Park. That project involved clearing some forty-seven acres of slums on the South Side and rebuilding the area with townhouses designed by I.M. Pei. Hyde Park is also known for Wright's Robie House, built in 1910 and one of the finest examples of Prairie School architecture. By the 1960s, the house was owned by the Chicago

Frank Lloyd Wright's Robie House, Chicago

Theological Seminary, which had decided to tear it down. Ever a champion of architects and good architecture, my father bought the Robie House and restored it for use as our construction and sales office. When we finished the Hyde Park project, Dad gave the house to the University of Chicago. A national historic landmark, it's now open to the public for tours.

While he was in Chicago, my father got to know Wright, so he invited the architect to dinner at his estate in Greenwich, Connecticut. Pei and his wife, Eileen, and I were also guests. From a design standpoint, I.M. and Wright were poles apart, but I.M. was polite to Wright and praised his work. But I could see right away that Wright had no use for Pei. After dinner, as we were going down to Dad's wine cellar—which Pei had designed—Wright fell on the stairs and had to be rushed to the hospital. I've always thought of that as Pei's revenge.

Working with my father was better training in planning and financing large-scale development than I ever would have gotten in business school. The empire he directed from his circular, Pei-designed penthouse office at 383 Madison Avenue was more ambitious than any developer would undertake today. Dad's reputation will live on forever. But his singular career came to an end in a spectacular fall that took a toll on him and everyone around him.

The two William Zeckendorfs, Jr. and Sr., 1964

My father was always extravagant. He loved travel and always went first class, reserving the best cabins on the great passenger liners for his frequent trips to Europe. In typical fashion, when he decided he wanted to build an underwater house off Eleuthera in the Bahamas, he hired Jacques Cousteau, the great marine explorer and conservationist, as a consultant. My father was also overextending himself professionally, leveraging properties at a ferocious clip. Less obvious was that he was in the

William Zeckendorf Sr. in his I.M. Pei–designed office at 383 Madison Avenue

grip of what we now believe was an undiagnosed bipolar disorder. The public only ever saw his manic side, though privately he was deeply depressed after Marion, his second wife, died in a plane crash. My father was by nature a generous man, but his rash spending on expensive toys and jewelry for his mistresses suggests that his manic states may have played a greater role in his professional demise than anyone realized.

With less and less equity in his projects, he would borrow at interest rates of close to 20 percent. As he became an easy mark for once sympathetic associates, the rates climbed even higher. Finally, he couldn't shuffle his deals fast enough. Unable to pay an $8.5 million credit call, Webb & Knapp went bankrupt in 1965. Having personally guaranteed many of the company's loans, my father was forced into personal bankruptcy three years later. His assets and the company's were lost.

While the bankruptcy proceedings were under way, I set up a new company, General Property Corporation, with Ronald Nicholson, a lawyer who was married to my sister and had worked for my father. Legally, my father wasn't allowed to participate in the new company, but he was very present as an unofficial advisor. Before her death, my stepmother Marion, for whom Dad had made a fair amount of money, gave us $100,000 to buy back our office furniture, which had been seized, and another $250,000 to get the new company on its feet. Metropolitan Life, which had also made money off my father over the years, offered to sell us the lease on 383 Madison, and the Manhattan Savings Bank, which occupied half the street frontage of the building, gave us the loan to make the purchase. The cost of the loan was a half-interest in the building, as well as the rents from all the tenants, including us. General Property would act as managing agent. We were back in business.

Bankruptcy hadn't dampened my father's genius for sniffing out deals. He steered us to the purchase and resale of the Manhattan Hotel, an older hotel on Eighth Avenue between West 48th and 49th Streets. At the time, foreign hotel companies were rushing to buy up properties in New York. I had been reading about an English group that was expanding, so I made a date to meet the chairman in London. All I took with me was a photograph of the hotel, but apparently that was enough. I sold him the Manhattan for a $6 million profit. It was the first money our new company made.

Later, I did a similar quick turnaround on the Airlines Terminal Building at Park Avenue and East 42nd Street, buying it and then selling it to Philip Morris as the site for a new headquarters. We made $2 million on that transaction.

Still, the fallout from the bankruptcy was horrendous. Webb & Knapp had employed almost five hundred people and had offices and properties across the country. All of it was gone. Our new company was a bare-bones operation with little capital and a staff of four—myself, my brother-in-law Ronald, a secretary, and my father as silent partner.

Just as we seemed to be turning a corner, we got a call from a loan officer at Chemical Bank. The bank was holding a check for $2 million signed by my father, but there weren't sufficient funds in the account to cover it. It turned out that Chemical and Chase had been passing the check back and forth between them for six months, each assuming my father was good for the money. Now Chase had finally refused to accept the check, and Chemical wanted us to pay up. I immediately covered the shortfall with a check from the General Property account, hand delivered to the bank.

My brother-in-law chose that moment to resign, and as an equal partner, he was entitled to take $2 million with him. The company was back on thin ice.

Not long after that, the company treasurer, who had worked for my father for many years, came to me in tears. We were in big trouble, he said. He hadn't paid our rent to Manhattan Savings for the past six months, and on top of that, he hadn't turned over the rents we were collecting from the other tenants in the building. Apparently, my father, to support his extravagant spending, had been going to the treasurer to cash checks, gradually drawing half a million dollars from the funds that should have gone to the bank. The treasurer and I looked at each other, fully aware of what this meant: criminal misappropriation, a felony.

I went downstairs right away and told the president of Manhattan Savings what had happened, then went back up to the office and ordered an independent audit to confirm exactly what we owed. I gave the bank our 50 percent equity in the building as a settlement and promised we would be scrupulous about turning over rents we collected in the future.

A few weeks later, while lunching with the senior lawyer for Manhattan Savings, our lawyer said how grateful he was that the matter had been settled to everyone's satisfaction without word getting out. The bank's lawyer told him that unfortunately that wasn't the case: banking regulations had required Manhattan Savings to report the matter to the Manhattan district attorney.

Within days, lawyers from the DA's office swarmed over our office to do their own audit. Our treasurer, comptroller, and comptroller's assistant were arrested, and I knew that the next finger would be pointed at me. No one in the DA's office would believe that I had had no knowledge of our company's misuse of funds.

Before I could be hauled off in handcuffs, I hired a criminal lawyer. A former assistant district attorney, he arranged a meeting with the DA's office. This would be my sole chance to explain myself. I was still in my mid-thirties, and I knew that an indictment would spell not just the end of our company but also the end of my career. If convicted, I could land in jail.

My appointment at the DA's office was scheduled for a Monday morning. It was one of the scariest days of my life. Accompanying me to the meeting were our company lawyer, who was a former dean of Columbia Law School, and Tex McCrary, who had managed my father's public relations for years.

We met in an office at 60 Centre Street. The three of us were seated on one side of the table, with several people from the DA's office on the other. I explained what had happened as best I knew. Apparently, they believed my story, because from that point on, I was viewed as a victim in the matter and escaped indictment. However, our treasurer and chief bookkeeper were indicted, as was my father, although in his case it was for failing to file his income tax.

My father, with his irrepressible optimism, had reacted to the bankruptcy of Webb & Knapp with an upbeat "This is great! Now we can start over." Sadly, he didn't get the chance. He had begun to suffer a series of strokes—perhaps another cause of his erratic behavior—from which he didn't recover before his death in 1976. But his spirits never faltered. In his retirement, my father, who had seldom had time for me when I was young, took delight in my boys. Like many grandparents, he became a doting playmate to his grandsons.

I've never been blessed with my father's optimism, however, and after I walked out of the DA's office, my spirits plummeted. Though I hadn't been indicted, I paid a price. Business came to a halt. I needed money desperately—and a change of scene.

At that point, Geoffrey Leeds came to my rescue. Leeds was a creative gadfly who'd had some dealings with my father. In 1961 Geoff opened the first disco in New York, L'Interdit, in the Gotham Hotel. A few years later he involved me in opening another disco, Shepheard's, in the Drake Hotel, which Dad then owned. Then in 1967, Geoff introduced me to Alfred Bloomingdale, chairman of Diners' Club, which at that time was a high-end credit card. I flew to Los Angeles to meet with Al. He had an unusual proposition: would I help the city of Long Beach, California, buy the *Queen Mary*—recently retired from the Cunard fleet—and bring the ocean liner to Long Beach to be turned into a tourist attraction? Bloomingdale thought the ship would brighten the industrial waterfront and be good publicity for Diners' Club. He was offering only expenses but hinted that a commission might be forthcoming. I agreed without a second thought. It sounded like fun, and I could use some of that after all I'd been through.

Geoff Leeds and I flew to London and checked into Claridge's. We met with the people from Cunard, who liked our plan to turn the *Queen Mary* into a hotel and provisionally agreed to sell. Bloomingdale, meanwhile, was pitching the idea to Long Beach, then an obscure small city newly rich from offshore oil drilling. Eventually, a delegation headed by Long Beach's mayor met with Cunard and bid on the ocean liner. After the bid was accepted, the *Queen Mary* made one last Atlantic crossing before sailing through the Panama Canal and north to California. I passed up a free trip but was on hand when the ship docked in Long Beach in 1967.

Queen Mary Hotel, Long Beach, California

London Bridge, Lake Havasu, Arizona

Though the *Queen Mary* was a luxury liner, the cost of converting her into a hotel was astronomical. Every pipe, every length of electrical wiring, indeed the entire infrastructure had to be replaced. Diners' Club left the project in 1970 when the company changed hands, but the hotel finally opened the next year. It remains a big draw for tourists.

After the publicity generated by the *Queen Mary* sale, the city of London decided to sell London Bridge, which was due to be replaced. Bob McCulloch, whose family owned Lake Havasu City, an enormous development in the Arizona desert, approached Al Bloomingdale about buying the bridge. Al again asked Geoff and me to take on the project. We contacted the London authorities but had a hard time convincing them our interest in the bridge was real.

Along with C. V. ("Woody") Wood Jr., who was going to promote the bridge, Bob joined us in England. First we had to figure out which bridge we were buying: London Bridge has a venerable history, but it isn't the more familiar Tower Bridge. McCulloch put in a bid for $2.46 million, and within a week, he was the proud owner of London Bridge. Stone by stone, the bridge was dismantled and shipped by sea to California, then trucked to Lake Havasu, where it was reassembled at a cost of $7 million. After the Grand Canyon, it's the most popular attraction in Arizona.

On My Own

By the early 1970s, my father had recovered from my stepmother Marion's untimely death and had remarried and moved in with his new wife. My wife, Nancy, and I moved into his old Beekman Place apartment, which we bought from Marion's estate. Nancy gave the place a much-needed sprucing up, installing air conditioning and restoring it to its former glory.

The year 1972 was a turning point for me. I had put the bankruptcy and its aftermath behind me and was finished acting as an agent for bits of British history. I was ready to return to real estate. From then on, I was on my own. General Property Corporation became Zeckendorf Company, and over the next decade I moved out from under my father's shadow and built a successful business renovating and reselling hotels in Manhattan. I became known for identifying undervalued properties, turning them around and adding value, then selling them at a profit.

Though business was good, I proceeded with caution. My father's implosion was never far from mind, and I was determined not to repeat his mistakes. I kept our office small, avoided publicity, and brought in equity partners on every deal. Most development deals require equity partners and bank financing. An equity partner is an investor who owns a fixed percentage of the development partnership and shares the profit and risk. A debt partner—usually a financial institution—lends money to the developer at a specific interest rate and doesn't participate in profits. The amount of equity put up by the partners determines how much money a bank will lend and at what interest rate. In the deals I put together, my equity partners were putting in all the money up front. I didn't have any money of my own to put up, but often I could bring in a savings bank or, later on, a Japanese investor, on the strength of my name.

In retrospect, the deals I made were not good for me personally. Basically, my partners got a free ride because of the institutional financing I brought in. They got their money out and still had a share in the project, whereas if the building went belly up, I was the one responsible for repaying the loan.

Moving Up

The Mayfair House

My father had an instinctive feel for the value of hotels. I think he appreciated that these older hotels were undervalued. Renovations didn't quite satisfy him on an intellectual level, but financially they were very successful projects.

WILLIAM LIE ZECKENDORF

By 1972, my father was out of the business altogether, but he still knew people and heard things. He tipped me off about the Mayfair House, my first big acquisition.

The Mayfair House was a small hotel at Park Avenue and East 65th Street. Handsome architecturally, it had a well-to-do clientele and Old World charm. But the building was almost fifty years old, and a look inside told me it had not been well maintained. It was being run as a residence hotel and was losing money. Given its prime location, however, it should have been bringing in as much as a full-service transient hotel. Even the hotel restaurant was hemorrhaging money.

Mayfair House, New York (top)

Sheldon S. ("Hack") Wilson, investment partner

Nancy and I decided to eat dinner in the restaurant to get a feel for the place. The restaurant could be entered only through the hotel lobby—our first tipoff that it wasn't very hospitable to diners. Then the maître d' didn't want to seat us. He acted as if the restaurant was for hotel residents only. When I finally persuaded him to let us in, I saw that every table that wasn't occupied had a reserved sign on it. I got the impression that the residents all had tables of their own, even if they weren't sitting at them at the moment.

We felt lucky to be seated—though not that lucky, as it turned out. The dining room was small and dingy and looked more like a teashop than an Upper East Side restaurant. The other diners were elegant but elderly, the roast beef special consisted of one thin slice, and the maître d' never did warm up. All in all, a lousy dinner. But that could be a positive, I figured: here was a chance to add real value. It wouldn't be hard to improve on the restaurant.

My father arranged for me to meet with John McGrath, chairman of the East New York Savings Bank, who was on the Long Island University board with Dad. We toured the Mayfair, and McGrath agreed to finance the purchase of the hotel and the improvements. New York was heading into a recession just then, and sales were slow and real estate cheap. Cheap, that is, if you could make the property turn a profit.

The seller was the estate of Jesse Jones, a wealthy Texas oilman who had been secretary of commerce under FDR. I wasn't the only bidder. But having seen the potential in converting it to a transient hotel and upgrading the premises, I bid higher. Not that I had any money to put into the deal: General Property, as our company was called at the time, was tapped out. But I knew an investor, Sheldon S. ("Hack") Wilson. Hack had owned the Pepsi-Cola bottling franchise in South Africa and in the early 1960s had moved to the United States. When I met him, he was president of Liebmann Breweries, maker of Rheingold Beer, and was investing in real estate on the side. With Hack's equity commitment and the backing of East New York Savings, I bought the hotel for $6 million.

Converting the Mayfair into a transient hotel didn't require major construction, just refurbishing the lobby, hallways, guest rooms, and baths. A concern in every conversion project is what to do with existing residents. Here we were lucky: most were happy enough to leave once they realized how much foot traffic transient guests would bring. But a few elected to stay. One was a woman whose apartment was directly above the one that had belonged to Jesse Jones. In the back of one of Jones's closets we found a door that opened to a staircase leading up to the woman's apartment. Turns out she had been Jones's longtime girlfriend, and in his will he had left her lifetime title to her apartment. We had to close off the staircase, but I still laugh when I think of Jesse Jones ducking into his closet and dashing upstairs to see his mistress. Only in New York. Or maybe Paris.

It was the Mayfair restaurant that interested me most, however, and after we closed on the hotel, we got a break in that regard. The hotel had been leasing a ground-floor office to a doctor who decided to move out. Conveniently, the office was next to the hotel kitchen and had its own entrance on East 65th Street. Adding the office to the existing facility would give us enough space for a proper restaurant.

We began construction on the restaurant before we even had a chef or manager. It was unheard of for a hotel restaurant to compete with New York's top establishments, but that's what I hoped to do. I interviewed a number of restaurant owners and chefs without any luck. Then one night at dinner with the bandleader and pianist Peter Duchin, I mentioned my wish to open a great restaurant in the hotel. Later that week, Peter called and said he knew just the person: Sirio Maccioni. My father and I knew Sirio from his days as maître d' at the Colony restaurant, which had recently closed. The Colony had been one of the two best restaurants in New York, with an elite clientele that was exactly what I wanted for the Mayfair.

Sirio Maccioni in front of his restaurant, Le Cirque

Sirio knew everyone, and everyone knew him. We talked. He had just one non-negotiable condition: it had to be *his* restaurant, with no interference from the hotel. That made perfect sense to me. We settled on the amount he would need to take over the space, and I cosigned his loan. Since I knew that most restaurants fail within the first year, I offered him a year rent-free. And since I wanted him to stay if the restaurant survived, I promised him a low rent thereafter.

Then I introduced Sirio to Ellen Lehman McCluskey, an interior designer known for her hotels and restaurants. Daughter of a Wall Street titan and grandniece of a former governor of New York, she was very much an insider in New York society. I told her, "Design a restaurant where you and your friends would want to eat." Sirio, who had heard a young socialite refer to Paris nightlife as a "circus," suggested naming the restaurant Le Cirque. Ellen came up with a playful and charming motif of amorous circus monkeys. The design delighted Sirio, as it would delight customers for years to come.

Every project has a snag somewhere. At the Mayfair, it was the neighbor next door, who objected to our using the 65th

Street entrance for the restaurant, convinced it would disturb the quiet ambiance of the block. Never mind that 65th Street was already a busy crosstown thoroughfare with a steady stream of automobile traffic. We described the sort of restaurant we planned, but the neighbor threatened to sue regardless. In the end there was no suit, but we made sure to design a handsome entrance with an unobtrusive canopy.

Sirio hired Jean Vergnes, who had been the chef at the Colony, for Le Cirque, and my father contributed some important Burgundies to the wine cellar. La Confrérie des Chevaliers du Tastevin, the wine society to which Dad and I belonged, held a private preview dinner to launch the room—and help shove the banquettes into place. (The installation crew hadn't finished on time.) Ellen McCluskey hosted an official opening party the next night. Le Cirque was an immediate success, and I credit it with turning the Mayfair House into a fine hotel. Any disruption the restaurant may have caused on East 65th Street now came in the form of U.S. presidents, global business leaders, famous artists, and the socially prominent of every stripe.

In 1997, after nearly twenty-three years at the Mayfair, Sirio moved Le Cirque to the Palace Hotel, and in 2004, he moved it again, to Bloomberg Tower on East 58th Street. Over the years, world-class chefs like Daniel Boulud have presided over the Le Cirque kitchen, and Sirio has opened restaurants around the world. Through it all, he has remained a close friend. When Nancy and I visited Sirio in Montecatini Terme, his birthplace in Tuscany, people came out of the shops and said, "You're Mr. Zeckendorf, and you're the one who helped Sirio. You were so good to him."

Saved by a Dog

Hotel Delmonico

What Bill had—and I've never met anyone who had it so completely—was that in his head he knew most of the key areas of New York. He knew the ins and outs, the buildings, who was involved in them, the stories, the legal structures they were under, the ways to transform them—things like that. So Bill could look at a property and determine whether or not a deal could be done. He could look at a project and see its enhanced value. Whereas someone else would look at the property and say, "How am I going to make any money if I have to pay you that kind of money?"

JUSTIN COLIN, investment partner

Even before Le Cirque had opened, my father, newly separated from his third wife, moved into the Mayfair. Indirectly, he figured in my next hotel purchase as well. In 1975, Sarah Korein, a prominent real estate investor who knew my father and was aware that I had purchased the Mayfair, contacted me through

Ed Lewis, a hotel broker. Mrs. Korein was planning to buy the Hotel Delmonico at the corner of Park Avenue and East 59th Street—another elegant location, if not quite as elegant a hotel as the Mayfair—and she wanted me to oversee renovation of the hotel and then manage it.

Sarah Korein, real estate investor

Built in 1929, the Delmonico had never been remodeled. It was losing money badly, Mrs. Korein told me, and it needed work. The owner-manager, David Phillips, who lived in the hotel, was in his nineties and ready to retire. His daughter, Gladys Altman, was raising a family in the suburbs and had no interest in taking over. They were anxious to sell, and Mrs. Korein thought the price—just under $7 million—was fair.

Here was another property with good potential for improvement. Mrs. Korein had already worked out the terms of purchase and was ready to put up the money. In return for my involvement, she would make me a partner in the deal. I wouldn't have to put up any money. Despite the success of the Mayfair, we hadn't yet turned a profit, and I badly needed another project. Participation without equity was very appealing. I decided to accept her offer.

I had always admired the exterior of the Delmonico, and I knew it had celebrity residents like Mary Martin and Ed Sullivan. But I had never been inside. When I took a look, I saw that most of the work it needed would be cosmetic. The books, however, were as discouraging as Mrs. Korein had said. The Delmonico was being run as a transient hotel with a few residential apartments. The guest rooms were drawing steady business, but in the two years since we had bought the Mayfair, the New York City economy had continued to deteriorate, and transient business wasn't likely to increase enough to improve revenues. The Delmonico would do better as a residential property, I figured. The guest rooms could easily be converted into luxury rental apartments.

Sarah Korein and I arranged to meet for lunch before going to her lawyer's office to close the sale. She was to give the sellers a deposit of $250,000. But at lunch she told me she had

Hotel Delmonico, New York

decided not to buy the Delmonico after all. She didn't have a good feeling about it. Mrs. Korein was small and delicate with a kindly smile, but behind her grandmotherly manner was one of the toughest negotiators I've ever encountered. No question, she meant what she said.

By then, however, I'd spent a lot of time studying the Delmonico, planning what to do with it and calculating costs and returns. I *did* have a good feeling about the hotel, and I wanted to buy it. But I didn't have $250,000. In fact, I didn't have a dime. I was in the process of selling our apartment on Beekman Place just to cover our living expenses.

I asked Mrs. Korein if she would mind if I took over the deal. She said no, so after lunch I went on to the closing alone, without any money in hand.

When I got to the lawyer's office for the closing, everyone was there. I told Mr. Phillips and Mrs. Altman that Mrs. Korein had pulled out but that I wanted to go through with the purchase myself. I would just need a few days to line up a partner and the $250,000 deposit. Absolutely not, said Mr. Phillips and his daughter. They had worked out a deal with Sarah Korein, and they didn't know me from Adam. It was Friday afternoon, the day before Passover, and the lawyers were in their yarmulkes, ready to go home for the holiday.

I used the office phone to call Hack Wilson, who was in California, and told him I had another hotel for us to buy if he could come up with $250,000 right away. He could, he said, but it wouldn't arrive until Monday. That wasn't good enough for the owners. I begged them to be patient a little longer.

While everyone waited, stone-faced, I called a potential investor I'd been introduced to by my wife. Nancy had been a principal ballerina for the Metropolitan Opera before our marriage, and at the moment she was working as a right hand to Lucia Chase, the artistic director of American Ballet Theatre. An ABT board member, Justin Colin—a retired investment banker who managed his wife's family's investments—had told Nancy he knew the Zeckendorfs by reputation and was prepared to invest with me if I ever had a suitable project. I crossed my fingers he would make good on his word, and he did. He promised I'd have the money on Monday.

Still that wouldn't do. Mrs. Altman was gathering her things to leave, too distracted to pay any more attention to me. Apparently, her family's beloved German Shepherd had been killed by an automobile, and all she could think of was how unhappy her young son was. She had to rush home and find a German Shepherd for the boy.

German Shepherd?

My father had a German Shepherd named Mozart who lived with him at the Mayfair. Trained as a police dog, he was so protective of Dad that he had attacked several maids. There was talk that the dog was about to be banished from the hotel. I called my father right away and asked, "Would you pledge your German Shepherd as a guarantee on the purchase of the Hotel Delmonico?"

I don't remember his exact response; he probably burst out laughing. But first thing the next morning he drove up to Mount Kisco in his chauffeured limousine and delivered Mozart to Gladys Altman. The Delmonico was mine.

That Monday, with equity commitments from Hack Wilson and Justin Colin, I went to Manufacturers Hanover, where my father knew the chairman and I knew the senior people in the real estate division. The bank gave me a loan for the balance of the purchase price. We were in business.

As part of my contract with Hack and Justin, Nancy and I got a rental apartment on the twenty-eighth floor of the Delmonico. We later moved to a thirty-first-floor apartment with spectacular city views. Nancy is as talented a designer as she is a dancer, and she managed to round up enough furniture and artwork from the vacant guest rooms to furnish the thirty apartments we had cobbled together. When we offered the apartments, they rented quickly—a big help financially.

Just as the restaurant at the Mayfair House had provided a chance to add some value, there were two unused spaces at the

Justin Colin, investment partner

Entrance to Régine's (top)

Clubgoers at Régine's

Delmonico—an abandoned ballroom on the ground floor and another room nearby—that represented a golden opportunity. I sensed possibilities but had no idea what they might be.

As it happened, Justin Colin had been studying auction houses, specifically Sotheby Parke Bernet & Co., as a potential investment for his family. And coincidentally, a friend had told me that the British auction house Christie's was interested in opening a New York branch. Intuitively, I felt an auction house would be the right use of the space, and Justin, with his knowledge of the field, agreed.

We rented the ballroom to Christie's, then carved out more space for them on the floor above, installing a connecting stairway and elevator. The Delmonico location proved successful for Christie's. And having two major auction houses on the Upper East Side—Sotheby's was just blocks away—increased sales for both and made auction weeks an important part of New York's social season. The Delmonico profited accordingly.

The French singer and nightclub manager Régine Zylberberg took the other empty space on the ground floor for her club, Régine's. As part of the deal, she also got the small penthouse apartment. I set up an office in two rooms on the fourth floor of the hotel. As our company grew, we took over more rooms, but we stayed at that location for another decade, until I built Delmonico Plaza, an office building, around the corner on East 59th Street.

I later had second thoughts about converting the Delmonico to apartments. It probably would have been more profitable as a hotel once the market turned around and tourism picked up again. But I did what seemed right at the time.

In 1981, we sold the Delmonico for $32 million, a tidy profit. The buyer? Sarah Korein.

A Nightmare

The McAlpin

The hotels don't get talked about a lot, but they were very important. The McAlpin did a lot to revitalize Herald Square.

WILLIAM LIE ZECKENDORF

After a series of strokes, my father died in 1976. It was not unexpected, but we had been close, and it hurt. I missed him a lot and still do. I didn't have much time to mourn, however. My hotel broker, Ed Lewis, was back with another project, the massive old McAlpin Hotel on Herald Square. Access to transportation is one of the first things I look for in a building, and the McAlpin was well located: Herald Square is a major subway hub and Penn Station is just a block away.

When it was built in 1912, the McAlpin was the largest hotel in the world. Its ornate Beaux-Arts style was popular among famous New York hotels of the day like the Biltmore and the Roosevelt. The twenty-five-story building had been renovated

McAlpin Hotel, Herald Square, New York

in the 1930s, but by 1976 it was run-down and losing money, which made it affordable. With Justin Colin, I bought the hotel for $2.5 million. We brought in Starrett, a company in which Justin's in-laws had a controlling interest, as an equity partner and our construction firm. Starrett arranged our financing, a Federal Housing Administration mortgage. We were eligible for the government-guaranteed mortgage because we were creating rental units.

The McAlpin had something like 1,500 guest rooms but only about a dozen rent-controlled tenants. I figured we could easily work around them. We weren't planning to turn the McAlpin into a luxury address, just to create clean, efficient apartments for middle-class New Yorkers. We knew the infrastructure needed updating, but the condition of the building turned out to be far worse than expected. This would be no simple refurbishing job. It was a disaster from day one.

We had budgeted for replacing the plumbing, electrical wiring, and air conditioning. But when we started stripping off wallpaper, we found that half the walls underneath were rotted out. Every time we turned around, something else needed replacing. As the work escalated, the completion date kept moving later. Meanwhile, the interest on our loan was steadily increasing, and eventually we were forced to borrow more.

One of the challenges in a renovation is something most people don't think about: you have little control over the construction workers. When a new building goes up, construction proceeds in orderly fashion, floor by floor. The sides of the floors remain open, so you can readily see who's doing what, and where and when. But in a renovation, at any given time workers are all over the building, hard to track. We found that some of them were hiding in the rooms, literally sleeping on the job.

Existing occupants can be a challenge in a hotel renovation. We had to shuffle around the McAlpin's long-term residents while we worked on their apartments. That was an inconvenience we had expected, but it was nothing compared to what we faced when one resident refused to budge. Because we were rewiring and replumbing the entire building, we needed access to every room. It reached the point where we offered the hold-out $1 million to move. Still she refused. We ended up building a temporary box around her whole unit—in effect, a little house—so we could work above, below, and on either side of her.

Finally, by 1980, we had close to seven hundred sparkling new apartments, mostly studios and one-bedrooms. Leasing went well, which was a huge relief. But in converting the McAlpin I got to see firsthand why the biggest cost overruns in building are generally associated with renovations.

My growing reputation as a specialist in hotel renovation led to one of the strangest encounters of my career. Just as we were about to start renovating the McAlpin I got a call from a Colonel Pak, a retired Korean Army officer. I couldn't imagine what he wanted, but I agreed to meet him the next day. It turned out that Colonel Pak was representing the Reverend Sun Myung Moon, founder of the Unification Church. He had something he wanted to discuss with me. Would Nancy and I visit the Reverend and Madame Moon at their estate in Tarrytown? Intrigued, I said yes.

They sent a car and driver to pick us up. We got to the Moon estate around midday and were greeted warmly. As we sat around drinking fruit juice, Reverend Moon said he wanted to become closer to the Jewish business community in New York. Would I introduce him? I told him I probably wasn't the right person for that, but I would do what I could. Moon changed the subject: he wanted to buy a hotel. Did I know of one for sale? I thought of the McAlpin: selling the building would be better for us financially than converting it to rental apartments. Then Reverend Moon declared that he wanted to leave for the city immediately to buy a hotel. Colonel Pak organized a caravan of seven Cadillac limousines, with Reverend Moon, Colonel Pak, Nancy, and me in the first car. As I directed the driver down Broadway, I noticed that the caravan was getting special attention from the traffic police.

New Yorker Hotel, New York (left)

Reverend Moon addresses Unification Church members in the grand ballroom of the New Yorker Hotel

We arrived at the McAlpin and got out of the car. Reverend Moon glanced at the outside of the hotel, then looked west down 34th Street. Pointing to a tall building, he asked, "Is that a hotel?" It was the New Yorker, which had been closed for some time and was in bad shape. "I will buy the New Yorker," Moon announced. "What is the price?" I made a call the next day and was told that the 2,500-room hotel was selling for $5 million—a fair price, given its sorry condition.

Reverend Moon closed on the New Yorker within thirty days and set his followers to work modernizing the building. When it was ready, they filled the rooms. A decade or so later, the hotel's grand ballroom drew media attention as the site of Moon's mass wedding for four thousand Unification Church members.

I didn't get anything out of the deal, but Nancy received three dozen white long-stemmed roses from the reverend.

Easy Money

The Statler Hilton

In those early summers when I worked for him, my father was building a hotel portfolio that included the Delmonico, Mayfair, and Statler Hotels. He obsessed over the operations, back of house, and occupancy statistics. He did spectacularly well renovating these hotel properties, improving operations, and then selling for a huge profit.

WILLIAM LIE ZECKENDORF

I was a real estate developer, not a hotelier, and my goal in buying hotels wasn't to operate them but to fix them up, sell them as soon as possible, and turn a profit. In 1978, I sold the Mayfair House to Regent Hotels for $11 million. At the Delmonico, Christie's and Régine's weren't yet up and running, and we were still renovating the McAlpin, but Ed Lewis, the broker who had steered me to those hotels, called about another one, the Statler Hilton. Back in 1954, my father had tried to buy the entire ten-hotel Statler chain for $67 million, but the owner,

Conrad Hilton, turned him down. I figured I'd have better luck buying just one of his hotels.

Formerly the Hotel Pennsylvania, the Statler was in a prime location, just across Seventh Avenue from Madison Square Garden and Penn Station. The building is a handsome McKim, Mead & White design. But it dates back to 1919, and like the Mayfair and the Delmonico, the building wasn't in good shape when I saw it. That brought the price within our range. Not many investors wanted to take on old hotels with their attendant headaches: aging mortgages, insufficient rent rolls, rent-controlled tenants, and messy construction. None of that fazed me, though.

Beyond its affordable price, the Statler had another virtue: there were very few residents living in rent-controlled apartments. Nearly the entire hotel could be converted to market-rate apartments.

Rent control is a peculiarly New York phenomenon that's often a stumbling block for real estate developers. It came into force during World War II to protect tenants from landlords who wanted to impose massive rent increases. People lucky enough to have rent-controlled apartments often sit on them for years, since controlled rents are much, much lower than the market rate. By the 1970s, many older hotels had converted some of their guest rooms into rental apartments to increase their income; rent regulations had changed so that those apartments were no longer under rent control and could be leased at market rate. Since nearly all of the apartments at the Statler were decontrolled, we wouldn't have to worry about the expense of relocating tenants or the hassle of working around them.

With equity from Justin Colin and Hack Wilson, and a loan from Manufacturers Hanover, I bought the Statler from the Hilton chain in 1979 for $24 million. We renovated the rooms and, four years later, sold it to two New York real estate investors, Abraham Hirschfeld and Arthur Cohen, at a profit of $22 million. It was only after the sale that I discovered value in the property that the buyers had seen but I had missed. The hotel lobby was several floors above street level, and the floors in

Vintage postcard of Hotel Statler, New York

between consisted of commercial space. Hirschfeld and Cohen realized that the commercial floors could be sold off separately from the rest of the hotel, and then the profits could be used to pay down the initial loan. I made a mental note to remember that for future deals.

The only hiccup in the sale of the Statler was that Hirschfeld asked for more time to put together his part of the financing. I was moving on and was ready to be relieved of the interest on our bank loan, so at first I wasn't in the mood to give him any leeway. But then I remembered that Hirschfeld had made his fortune in parking garages—a notoriously rough business with rumored mob connections—and I'd heard he was not a man who made idle threats. (He was later convicted of trying to hire a hit man to bump off one of his former partners.) When Hirschfeld repeated his request for more time, I couldn't say yes fast enough.

Win Some, Lose Some

The Navarro, the Barbizon, and the Shoreham

Looking back now, it should have been obvious that a man so creative would never be content renovating someone else's building.

WILLIAM LIE ZECKENDORF

The Mayfair, the Delmonico, the McAlpin, and the Statler were my largest hotel conversions. But in the 1970s and early 1980s, I was involved in three other hotel deals for better or worse.

The Hotel Navarro on Central Park South was an upscale 260-room hotel with a stately appearance but a colorful history. It was a haven for celebrities: during the 1970s, rock bands like the Rolling Stones, the Grateful Dead, the Kinks, and the Who made the hotel their New York headquarters, and Bruce Springsteen lived there for a while. The stories are legion. One time our accountant got a bill from the hotel. It seems the Who's drummer, Keith Moon, had become so frustrated when he couldn't get into his sound engineer's room next door that he had taken a hammer and chisel and punched his way, brick by brick, through the adjoining wall.

Our plan was to convert the Navarro into a condominium. But in 1980 when John Coleman, who owned the Ritz-Carlton in Washington, D.C., offered us $15 million, we sold it. Coleman renamed it the Ritz-Carlton.

Barbizon Hotel, New York

One purchase I later regretted was the Barbizon on East 63rd Street and Lexington Avenue. For years it had been a women's hotel, an upscale SRO for proper young ladies moving to New York. The roster of women who lived at the Barbizon back in the day was a "who's who" of the arts, from actresses Lauren Bacall, Grace Kelly, Candice Bergen, and Liza Minnelli to writers Joan Didion, Sylvia Plath, Ann Beattie, and Eudora Welty. The rooms were tiny, and the bathrooms were down the hall—just like the college dorms many of the young women had only recently left.

By the 1970s, liberated women weren't interested in being chaperoned, and the Barbizon was losing money. But the Upper East Side location was good, and the building was distinctive architecturally, blending Italian Renaissance, Gothic, and Islamic elements. So in 1979, I bought the hotel for $7 million, with a rich Australian as my equity partner. It seemed like a sure bet to convert the building into apartments or a transient hotel catering to male as well as female guests.

Unfortunately, the Barbizon turned out to be a financial sinkhole, with construction problems from the start. We were also stuck with a dozen or so rent-controlled residents who wouldn't move. I concluded that we were in a bad situation and should sell, but it took some time to persuade my Australian partner. I still think I did him a big favor in getting us out of the project: the people who bought it from us went bankrupt.

One of my biggest disappointments during those years was the Shoreham, a hotel in Washington, D.C., that Justin Colin and I bought in 1979 for $35 million. We planned to refurbish the rooms of this once prestigious hotel, but the real draw was the land behind it, which overlooked Rock Creek Park. We wanted to build luxury condominiums on the site and commissioned David Childs of Skidmore, Owings & Merrill to draw up plans. But after protracted negotiations and revision of our plans, we couldn't get the necessary approvals. We fixed up the hotel and were finally able to unload it in 1984 to VMS Realty, a Chicago firm, but we'd lost a lot of money on it by then.

These things happen: projects that look good on paper for one reason or another don't pan out. But the Shoreham was an opportunity I was particularly sorry to lose. A lot of energy had gone into the planning, and David had put together a good design. Years earlier, my father had been frustrated in his efforts to complete a massive redevelopment project in southwest Washington, and I didn't like being similarly disappointed.

The Visionary

By the end of the 1970s, I'd had enough of rehabbing old hotels and the headaches that entailed. I was ready to build.

Working for my father, I'd seen the power of development to change neighborhoods and improve lives. Kips Bay, the ground-breaking apartment complex in Midtown Manhattan that was I.M. Pei's first residential design, was followed by neighborhood changers in Philadelphia, Pittsburgh, Chicago, and Denver, where Dad's commercial redevelopment downtown included the city's first new office building since World War II.

Park West Village, the apartment complex my father built between West 97th and 100th Streets as part of Title I, a government-subsidized plan to replace slum housing, was intended to launch the revitalization of the West Side above 86th Street. But after it opened to much fanfare in 1960, development in the area ground to a halt until the early 1980s. That's when I got my first shot at developing something of my own from the ground up, at Broadway and West 96th Street.

I knew the Upper West Side well, having grown up on Central Park West at 88th Street and later on 67th Street between Central Park West and Columbus Avenue. Central Park West was safe, but in the early 1980s upper Broadway and the side streets were still pretty rough.

All that was about to change. My vision was to develop the Broadway corridor from West 96th Street down to 14th Street.

I started at the top.

Opening the Broadway Corridor

The Columbia

People called the Columbia "Zeckendorf's Folly" and said, "You're crazy. That's the demilitarized zone: too dangerous, too remote."

LAWRENCE ADAMS, architect and former associate in Frank Williams's office

In 1981, the Starrett Corporation, our construction firm on the McAlpin, tipped me off to a site at Broadway and West 96th Street. The site had a checkered history. Efforts to build branches of Alexander's and Gimbels department stores had failed, and a proposal for mixed-income housing had been squelched by the community. The property languished until Starrett, one of the largest builders of apartment houses in the city, bought the one-acre lot in 1977. Starrett took a stab at developing the property on their own, hiring an architect to draw up plans for a residential high-rise. But before they could break ground, the company hit a bigger snag: the Iranian Revolution.

Starrett had been building a large apartment project in Tehran, but when the shah was deposed, the property was seized by the new government. Suddenly the company was out some $112 million. While Starrett's chairman, Henry Benach, was in Europe pursuing the company's claim against Iran, back in New York they were scrambling for cash. One day Justin Colin invited me to the Starrett offices. Benach, Justin told me, had proposed that I take over development of the West 96th Street site.

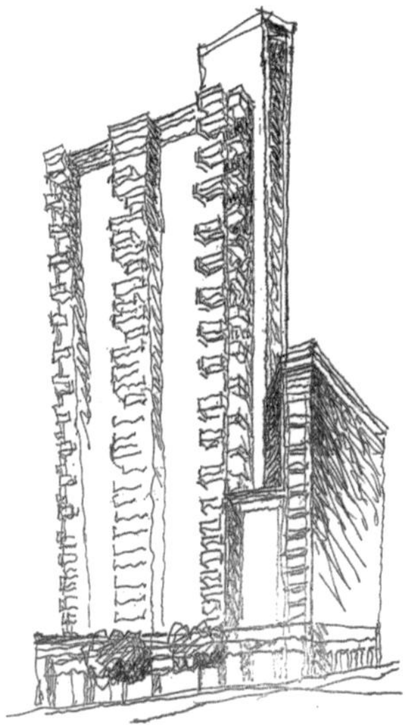

Sketch of the Columbia by architect Frank Williams

There were good reasons to say yes. It was a large site—30,000 or 40,000 square feet—and it was empty. There would be no tenants to relocate, no building to tear down. There was excellent access to transportation, and the zoning allowed for an ample FAR, or floor area ratio. The FAR determines the total square footage allowable on a lot and thus how high a building can go. The FAR for our site meant that we could build big as of right—that is, no special zoning variances would be required. Big is key for turning around a decaying neighborhood. A small building won't change anything; the infusion of high-quality new apartments must be sufficient to upgrade the available housing stock. We added floors to Starrett's original plans and came up with a 400,000-square-foot, 32-story tower with 303 apartments.

Starrett gave me a fair price for the land. I could have tried to negotiate, but they needed the money and the work. New York was going through a building slump, so the construction trades—ironworkers, electricians, concrete workers—came in with lower-than-usual bids.

Manufacturers Hanover gave us a loan for land and construction, but because of the risky location, the bank insisted I bring in high equity participation. Justin Colin was absorbed in other parts of his business, and Hack Wilson had backed off real estate investment at the time, so I had to pull in other partners. I had a referral to Lincoln Savings Bank, which agreed to come in as an equity partner. But since equity partners come after principal lenders in recovering funds if a project fails, they carry more risk. So Lincoln charged us higher interest on their loan

View of the Columbia, New York, from the opposite corner of Broadway and West 96th Street

than Manufacturers Hanover was charging us. On the plus side, the site was essentially ready for construction and we had a set of plans in hand, so we figured we could finish building quickly and pay off our loans. I went ahead and signed an agreement with Lincoln.

The building was not only my first foray into ground-up construction but also my sons' initiation into the real estate business.

Will, my elder son, worked alongside me before going to Santa Fe to help out on a condo project I had undertaken and later to Harvard Business School. Arthur came aboard when Will left, assisting our project manager through the construction phase.

I can't say the community was bowled over by the news that we planned to put up condominiums. We hired Edith Fisher, who had extensive experience leading neighborhood groups, to meet with community members and assure them that our intentions were good. Edith proved to be such an invaluable community liaison that we hired her full time. She stayed with us for many years, eventually becoming a vice president of the company.

One major obstacle was a community garden on the site—a local institution. We promised the gardeners they could stay until we were ready to break ground. They had a better idea: that we make the garden a part of the new building. Initially we proposed erecting a greenhouse on the roof of our parking garage, but the gardeners nixed that, afraid that debris thrown from an SRO hotel next door would shatter the glass. Instead, we decided to spread a one-and-a-half-foot layer of soil on the roof and install adequate drainage.

The issue then was what would happen to the plants in the community garden while the building was under construction. My son Arthur came up with an ingenious solution. He arranged to move the entire garden, plant by plant, to a stretch of Riverside Park near West 91st Street. It's still flourishing there today. For the new garden on the garage roof, we gave the gardeners $25,000 along with a $50,000 allowance for ongoing support and a fifteen-year lease at $1 a year. In 1983, when the building opened, the garden community laid out the rooftop space. Today, the Lotus Garden, as they named it, is bursting with trees and shrubs, and individual plots are rented out for a nominal fee. The garden is even open to the public on Sunday afternoons from April to November, providing a quiet retreat from the urban hubbub.

Arthur also helped with another challenge: a rundown public restroom on the Broadway median at 96th Street. We worked

West 91st Street community garden, Riverside Park, New York

with the community to turn it into a station for the auxiliary police and offices for several civic organizations. Citibank and the Lila Acheson Wallace Foundation (set up by the founders of *Reader's Digest*) also contributed to the renovation.

We were just about to break ground when two unexpected zoning issues came up. I hired John Zuccotti, a deputy mayor under Abe Beame and head of the City Planning Commission for several years, to help resolve them. The first concern was our underground parking. I wanted the garage to open onto 96th Street, a major thoroughfare, to draw traffic coming off the West Side Highway, but that would have required a zoning variance. Despite Zuccotti's efforts, we had to relocate the entrance to 97th Street. In the end, it didn't matter: commuters found their way around the block.

The second zoning issue was more distressing. In the final plans, we had dedicated 16,000 square feet—practically the whole ground floor—to a health club with a pool. Health clubs were not a standard amenity in apartment buildings in those days, but we felt it would be important for attracting buyers. The club would also generate considerable income for the building, since we planned to open membership to the public. However, a commercial health club that had been in the neighborhood for years fought our plan and won. We had to move the club up several floors, eating up valuable space we could have sold for apartments, and we had to restrict the facility to building residents. Nevertheless, the health club was a good draw for sales, allowing us to raise the condo prices and common charges, which offset the loss of the income that a commercial facility would have generated.

The groundbreaking ceremony was a major event, attended by Mayor Ed Koch; Andrew Stein, the Manhattan borough president; and our good friends from the community board. We also had some unexpected participants: a group of protesters who tried to disrupt the proceedings by shouting and shaking the chain-link fence around the site. In those days, the Upper West Side from 90th Street to 110th was heavily politicized, with a strong radical bent. The protesters were violently opposed to our project, condemning it as an attempt to gentrify the neighborhood. They were right about that. Our building was the first new construction above West 96th offering market-rate housing, and it changed the face of the Upper West Side.

We named the building the Columbia in a nod to the nearby university. As a condominium it was a rarity in New York at the time; most non-rental residential buildings were cooperatives. Co-ops are structured as corporations: a buyer purchases shares in the corporation and in return receives a proprietary lease on an apartment. Condo buyers own their apartments outright, just as if the units were detached dwellings. Co-ops tend to carefully screen buyers, who are subject to all sorts of rules and regulations, while condos generally have far fewer restrictions, welcoming pretty much anyone who can afford to buy an apartment. A sales brochure for the Columbia outlined some of the advantages of a condominium: "A condominium owner is not required to assume a share of the entire building's underlying mortgage, as cooperative owners do. Condominium owners do not have to clear most decisions pertaining to the property with a board of directors. Unlike cooperative shareholders, you have almost complete freedom to sell or rent your condominium whenever you want."

The condo model had a distinct benefit for us as developers: we could sell the apartments, pay off our loans, and distribute the profits among the investment partners. The co-op model is advantageous for property owners who prefer to hang onto their assets, using them as a steady source of income. In the mid-1980s condos represented only 15 percent of the non-rental apartment market in Manhattan; now about 25 percent of non-rentals are condos.

Frank Williams, architect of the Columbia

We decided to hire an outside agent, J. I. Sopher, to sell the apartments, since we lacked the experience to market them ourselves and there were no comparable buildings in the area to guide us in setting prices. We didn't want to overprice the units and risk having the building stand empty while interest mounted on our loans, so we decided to stimulate interest by selling the studios low, at $150 a square foot. But even before they went on sale, I lowered the price to $100 a square foot. When the sales office opened the first day, there were lines down the block, and the studios sold out in six hours. We probably could have sold them for more, but the excitement generated by the sales carried over to the larger units, and the entire building sold in six months. We also leased out the street-level commercial space quickly and sold the parking concession to one of the city's larger companies.

Not every sale closes without a hitch, and some sales fall apart altogether. The owner of a Chinese restaurant arranged to buy one of the Columbia apartments in an all-cash deal. Cash transactions are good for the seller: you don't have the buyer's financing to deal with. But our Chinese buyer apparently took "all-cash" literally. The day of the closing, I got an urgent phone call from our attorney: "The buyer's here, but instead of a check he's got a suitcase with $120,000 in cash. We can't take it." No loss to us; we had no problem lining up another buyer.

I always admired my father's commitment to fine architecture, and I was determined to continue the practice in my projects. At the Columbia I was working with plans commissioned by Starrett, and I wasn't keen on the design. I found it a little too

Princeton House, New York

blocky, although the cantilevered balconies create some visual excitement on the facade. I also wasn't crazy about the yellowish color of the brick. But at least the building wasn't one of those cookie-cutter white-brick high-rises that sprang up all over New York in the 1950s and 1960s. And when I met the architect, Frank Williams, I liked him immediately: he was young, smart, and capable. The Columbia was the first of many projects we worked on together. Frank became, in effect, my house architect, my I.M. Pei.

Financially, the Columbia was very successful. It cost $55 million to build, and we easily reached our target of a 20 percent profit. The moderate pricing opened up ownership to a broad market. Several Broadway actors bought in early on. Not only did they like being a short subway ride from the theater district, but as one actress, now retired, observed, it is only because her condo was so affordable thirty years ago that she has been able to continue living in Manhattan.

Initial buyers weren't the only people who benefitted. What the Columbia did for the Broadway corridor was miraculous. Within a few years, every available site south of 96th Street was under construction. In fact, one new building, a block below the Columbia, was mine. I had a minority position in Princeton House, a seventeen-story condo with 212 units, designed by Schuman Lichtenstein Claman Efron. A 1984 zoning law revision limited the height of new buildings on the Upper West Side in an effort to preserve the character of the neighborhood through "contextual" design. When Princeton House opened in 1985, Paul Goldberger, architecture critic for the *New York Times*, commended it for its compatibility with the older buildings around it.

Transformation of the Upper West Side was under way. I was off to a good start.

Looking Up

The Park Belvedere

The transferability of air rights became one of Bill's greatest talents. He could look at a building and figure out how he could transfer the air rights to whatever he wanted to build.

JUSTIN COLIN, development partner

In October 1983, shortly after the Columbia opened, I was on a panel at a community meeting called to discuss future development on the Upper West Side. In order to maintain the area's distinctive character, the City Planning Commission was proposing to add height restrictions to the zoning laws. Most of the architects, planners, historians, and city officials at the meeting were in favor of them, and in fact, the new zoning regulations went into effect in 1984. But I spoke up to oppose height limits, arguing that the likely result would be buildings that were less desirable to live in. Under the new laws, for example, the Columbia would have been limited to twenty-two stories instead of thirty-two.

At the time of the meeting, we had already broken ground on a condominium at Columbus Avenue and West 79th Street, and I was accused of having fast-tracked those plans to avoid the height limit. True, we had moved quickly on the new building, but beating the rezoning was not the only incentive. Once your financing is in place, you don't want to delay construction. You're paying interest on your construction loan every day, whether or not any work is under way.

I remained convinced that high-rise development was a positive step for the Upper West Side, and other developers clearly agreed. But while the wave of new apartment construction was rolling down Broadway, Columbus Avenue was a different story. Columbus is just a block from Central Park West, one of the city's most fashionable residential areas. In the early 1980s, however, the avenue was still marginal, marked by crumbling brownstones, aging tenements, and rundown walk-ups. An exception was the four-block parklike oasis between 77th and 81st Streets where the American Museum of Natural History stands.

Across Columbus from the museum, on the northwest corner of 79th Street, sat the Park West Funeral Chapel. Like the adjacent brownstones along 79th, it was only five or six stories high. I started thinking: if I tore down the funeral home and bought air rights to the brownstones, I could put up a high-rise with views of Central Park, the Hudson River, and uptown and downtown Manhattan.

Air rights, or transferable development rights, were not a new concept in Manhattan at the time. The railroads had built platforms over their tracks and sold rights to the air space above them for projects like the Pan Am Building—now the MetLife Building—which straddles Park Avenue near Grand Central Station. But back in the 1980s, transferring air rights to build a residential tower was still a novel concept.

I went back to Frank Williams, the architect of the Columbia, and asked him to come up with a design. The Columbia was essentially middle-income housing, but I decided on a luxury building for the new site. Putting up a high-end residential

Belvedere Castle, Central Park, New York

tower on Columbus Avenue was a gamble, but given the proximity to Central Park West, I was confident it would work. We named our building the Park Belvedere—a reference to Belvedere Castle, a landmark in nearby Central Park.

By then, Justin Colin had bowed out of real estate investment. Once again it was Nancy who brought me a new partner. After she retired from the Metropolitan Opera ballet, Nancy continued to take ballet classes, studying with the Russian master Igor Schwezoff. She and a classmate, Sono Osato Elmaleh, would go to the Carnegie Deli for tuna fish sandwiches after class. Sono's husband, Victor Elmaleh—an auto distributor who was among the first to import Volkswagens to the United States—was interested in real estate investment. When Victor heard about my plans for the Park Belvedere, he approached me about becoming an equity partner. This was the first of many times I partnered with Victor and his company, World Wide Holdings.

Lincoln Savings Bank had already come in as an equity partner. So with Frank's plans and Victor's and Lincoln's equity in hand, I went to Manufacturers Hanover for purchase and construction loans. I paid $6 million for the funeral home and $1.7 million for the air rights to the neighboring brownstones. We broke ground on the Park Belvedere before we had even opened the

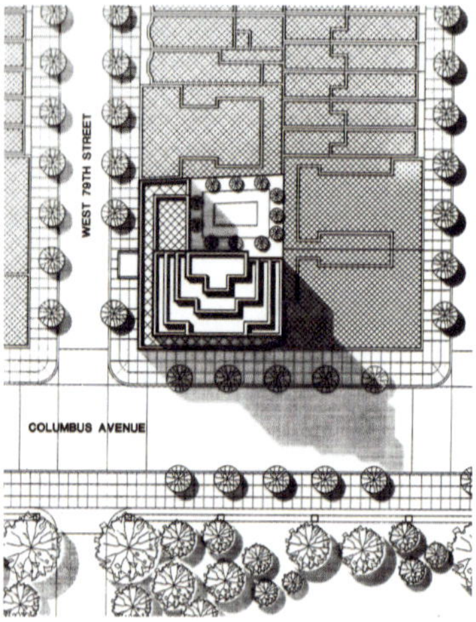

The Park Belvedere site plan (left)

The Park Belvedere, New York, under construction

View of the Park Belvedere from the southeast (opposite)

sales office at the Columbia—a risky decision. But as I watched the Columbia sell out soon after that, I was convinced we would have no problem.

The Park Belvedere was one of the first "sliver" buildings, rising thirty-five stories on a narrow 12,000-square-foot lot. With its slender tower and setbacks, it acknowledges classic Central Park West apartment houses like the San Remo, the Beresford, and the Majestic.

Not only did the handsome design incorporate traditional stylistic elements but the building was constructed using traditional structural methods. The concrete floors were laid according to time-honored techniques developed by the Italians who controlled the concrete trade in New York. It was poured on site into wooden frames, then once it had set—"cured," in construction lingo—the wooden frames were pulled away and reassembled for the next floor. Like most apartment buildings in New York, the Park Belvedere is clad in brick. Frank chose a salmon-colored brick that was larger and more textured than usual, giving the building an elegance in keeping with its neighbors along Central Park West.

The interior was as carefully conceived as the exterior. The 155 apartments were designed with meticulous attention to comfort and detail, with walk-in closets, high-end fixtures and finishes,

and top-of-the-line kitchen appliances. As a further amenity—one not offered before in a New York apartment building—the one- and two-bedroom units were laid out so they could be combined easily into larger apartments. This proved to be an effective marketing tool, and designing interiors so the apartments could be readily joined became a Zeckendorf trademark.

At the Columbia, we had hired J. I. Sopher to advertise and sell the apartments, but my sons thought we could do better marketing the Park Belvedere ourselves. Will and Arthur did a splendid job. We opened sales at $400 a square foot—a record high at the time. The condos sold briskly, and the street-level retail space was rented quickly.

We completed the Park Belvedere in 1985. As the first luxury apartment building on Columbus Avenue, it set the stage for the highly desirable residential area there today, with trendy restaurants, upscale boutiques, and family-friendly housing. The location is one of the best on the West Side, and the apartments have quadrupled in value.

Win-Win with the A&P

The Copley

My father was very good with property owners—very good at talking to them, getting to know them, gaining their confidence, and getting them to sell.

WILLIAM LIE ZECKENDORF

Other developers were watching the Columbia closely. Once it was clear the condos were selling, the rush was on to buy up any available property on Broadway. One site, on the northeast corner of Broadway and West 68th Street, caught my eye. My competitors had been steering clear of the lot because of its awkward shape. But the only structure on it was a two-story A&P. I figured I'd better move quickly before someone else saw its potential.

The lot was smaller than the Columbia's but larger than the Park Belvedere's. With a higher FAR, I wouldn't need to assemble quite as many air rights to build an apartment tower. I could transfer rights from a small church east of the site, on West 68th

The Copley, New York

View of the Copley from the opposite side of Broadway (opposite)

Street, and from the Spencer Arms, an ornate but dilapidated residential hotel to the north. First, though, I would have to get rid of the A&P.

That wasn't as easy as I'd hoped. The store was profitable, and the parent company figured business would only increase as development in the area picked up. We had endless meetings at the company's New Jersey headquarters, but management seemed more interested in running their supermarket than in making a big profit selling the land. Finally, after six months of negotiations, I came up with a solution. I would buy the property and demolish the supermarket, then build a new A&P-owned Food Emporium on the ground floor of the apartment tower I put up. Fine, said A&P, as long as they could specify the plans for the new store and lease it at a cheap rent. It took another year to negotiate the purchase price and the rent, but in the end, the deal was a win-win: I was able to acquire the site for practically nothing, and A&P got a brand new store and a favorable lease.

We didn't raze the A&P and break ground until construction was under way on the Park Belvedere and on a project I had in the works across town—Delmonico Plaza, an office building on East 59th Street. The A&P site offered great views up and down Broadway, so I wanted a strong design. I hired Lew Davis of Davis, Brody & Associates, who was also my architect on Delmonico Plaza and two other buildings.

Zoning laws mandated keeping or replacing any stores on the property: we met that requirement with the supermarket. Under the revised height regulations instituted in 1984, the blockfront of any new building could not be higher than that of the adjacent buildings. To maintain the uniform height, Lew designed a building with an eight-story base along Broadway and a twenty-eight-story tower rising from a setback on the ninth floor. To align the base with the brownstones on the 68th Street side, he designed a five-story blockfront with an opening for the supermarket's loading dock.

Small print in the zoning regulations aimed at encouraging "contextual sensitivity, enhanced safety, and on-site recreation

space" allowed us to add volume at the back of the building in exchange for elements like a community plaza on the roof of the supermarket and windows in the elevator lobbies. Setbacks gave many of the east-facing apartments Central Park views, and some had winter gardens—small, enclosed greenhouses that together formed a ribbon of dark-tinted glass cascading down the eastern face of the building. The rest of the facade consisted of horizontal bands of tan limestone alternating with bands of aluminum and glass.

Completed in 1987, the Copley was a critical success and the condos sold well, at much higher prices than those at the Columbia. Starrett was again our contractor, and construction proceeded smoothly. Once the new residents moved in, however, trouble hit. The aluminum-and-glass bands that looked so handsome developed leaks, and the windows started popping out of their frames. Repairs were extensive—and expensive.

Problems like those inevitably lead to a lot of finger pointing. First everyone blamed the window manufacturer, who in turn blamed the contractor for improper installation. The contractor then blamed the architect for faulty drawings. Unfortunately, as usually happens, blame came to rest on the developer, and we ended up with the expense of repairs. I thought about suing but decided it wasn't worth the time and lawyers' fees when the outcome was uncertain. Nearly every project involves overruns, and to cover the expense, developers hold money in reserve—$1 million was standard in those days. The Copley repairs cost us more, but because we were on time with construction and sales, we didn't lose money on the project.

The Spencer Arms Hotel was another matter. We had bought the whole building, not just the air rights, with plans to convert it into a transient hotel. There were too many longtime residents who wouldn't move, however, so we sold the hotel at a marginal profit.

Location, Location

Central Park Place

This project involved a very complex process of permitting, design, and construction that eventually resulted in one integrated building, though in fact Central Park Place is two separate buildings appearing as one. Overcoming such complexity was typical of Bill's development strategy of taking on sites that others regarded as too challenging.

TOM JAVITS, former senior VP and managing director, Zeckendorf Company

New York is a city of neighborhoods. In Manhattan, you can walk a few blocks east or west and find yourself in a completely different socioeconomic environment. This was especially true on the Upper West Side in the 1980s.

New building in the Lincoln Center area began around the time the performing arts complex opened in the 1960s. As part of Robert Moses's urban renewal program, my father developed Lincoln Towers, a twenty-acre residential complex that replaced

Vintage postcard of the New York Coliseum, Columbus Circle, New York

Central Park Place, New York (opposite)

a slum area to the west of Lincoln Center. By the early 1980s, a handful of other residential buildings had gone up nearby. But just a few blocks south, Columbus Circle was a wasteland.

Geographically, Columbus Circle is an important transportation hub at the southwest corner of Central Park, where Broadway, Central Park West, Central Park South, and Eighth Avenue converge. But the area was a dreary no-man's-land, stylistically closer to Hell's Kitchen, its neighbor to the south, than to the more prosperous stretches to the north and east. The circle itself was dominated by the New York Coliseum, the city's convention center. A squat 1950s white-brick box with a twenty-story office tower appended to it, the Coliseum, along with a housing development to its west, was an urban-renewal carryover from the Robert Moses era. It had served its purpose for nearly thirty years, but the immense new Jacob K. Javits Convention Center then going up on West 34th Street was about to put the Coliseum out of business.

I knew Columbus Circle would be pivotal in opening up the Broadway–Eighth Avenue corridor going south. While other developers were sniffing around the Coliseum, I started buying up property in the block just below it, at the northwest corner of West 57th Street and Eighth Avenue. I envisioned a mixed-use building occupying the entire blockfront on Eighth Avenue

East facade of Central Park Place

between 57th and 58th, with an apartment tower, a commercial base with offices and retail, and a hotel. There was nothing like it nearby.

It took me six years to put together the assemblage, which included a tenement and a couple of rundown nineteenth-century buildings containing small offices, shops selling cheap merchandise, and a Woolworth's. One by one, I relocated all the tenants and bought the buildings.

Then we hit a snag. On the north side of the block, along 58th Street, there was an eight-story, single-room occupancy hotel, the Alpine. Our plan called for tearing it down, but the city had just put a moratorium on demolishing SROs. After lengthy negotiations, plus a hefty payment to the city for replacement housing, we finally got permission to raze the hotel. But it came too late for us to proceed with our original scheme. We had already redrawn our plans for the tower on a smaller half-block footprint without the hotel lot and, in order to meet the deadline for a tax abatement, had begun laying the foundations for the revised design. So I transferred the air rights from the Alpine to the residential tower, adding ten stories.

Lew Davis was again our architect. He designed a fifty-five-floor tower with 274 apartments and a seven-story commercial base. The design was innovative in several ways. For one thing, the building—which we named Central Park Place for its proximity to the park—was one of the first residential projects in New York to use curtain-wall construction. A curtain wall is a non-load-bearing exterior wall. Curtain-wall construction does not require a heavy frame; instead, a skin of glass and/or lightweight material is applied to the exterior of the building. This allows for a much more creative design.

The distinctive sculptural profile of Central Park Place is defined on the exterior by bay windows that visually create vertical lines from base to cap. The five-sided bays give the apartments good light and views of Central Park and the city skyline. My son Arthur figured out the sight lines, and even the arrival of skyscrapers like the Time Warner Center to the north and Norman Foster's Hearst Tower to the south hasn't obscured the views.

For the skin of the building, Davis used aluminum, as he had at the Copley. But here, the windows remained intact. One of the most striking features of Central Park Place is the soft gray-green of the aluminum cladding. The green was intended to link the building to the park but I found the final result too pale. It looked washed out. Still, the use of color was daring and distinguished the building from its more conventional neighbors.

Overall, the critical response to Central Park Place was positive. Even the water tank on top of the building got a favorable review from journalist Carter Horsley: "For connoisseurs of water-tank enclosures, this tower boasts one of the city's prettiest, the perfect cap to this very modern 'pneumatic' tower."

HRH was our construction firm, and Manufacturers Hanover provided our construction loan. My equity partners were Omni Properties and KG Land, a division of Kumagai Gumi, a Japanese construction firm. This was the first project on which I partnered with Kumagai Gumi, but certainly not the last.

Given the booming Japanese economy in the early 1980s and the strength of the yen against the dollar, real estate companies and individual buyers from Japan were scooping up New York properties. Kumagai Gumi wanted in on the Central Park Place deal not just as an investment but also for the accounting benefit. Government contracts in Japan were awarded on the basis of the bidders' total billings, and they wanted to claim the full $135 million of our construction costs. I had no problem with that.

What I did have a problem with was that as part of our deal, KG Land was entitled to market the most desirable apartments in the building. This did not sit well with my two sons, who by then were in charge of sales and marketing for Zeckendorf projects. The consolation was that KG did much of their marketing in Japan. There was one idiosyncrasy in the Japanese market we had not encountered before: the Japanese favor south-facing apartments and those with the lucky number 8 in their address. We did our best to accommodate the buyers.

The rest of the building also sold well, and at record prices. The apartments, although not large, were well laid out, and the building's amenities included a fitness center—soon to become a standard feature in luxury high-rises.

Condos were still a novelty when Central Park Place went up, so to market the apartments we did something no one else was doing at the time, though it's standard practice now: we created a floor of model apartments so potential buyers could see exactly what the units would look like. Birch Coffey, an architect who was heading up the interiors department at Davis, Brody, designed the interiors of Central Park Place, including

4 Columbus Circle, the office building at Central Park Place

the model apartments. We liked his work, and when Nancy and I decided to do a major renovation of our apartment in the Hotel Delmonico, we asked Birch to take it on. Birch was very impressed with Nancy. "She was an absolute genius at figuring out storage possibilities," he said. "She designed a closet the way other people design a living room, using every square inch."

It would be another decade before the Columbus Circle area was fully gentrified, but with Central Park Place we at least got it started. Buyers who bought in at the beginning were rewarded with steep increases in the value of their apartments. The building attracted celebrities like Al Pacino, Gene Hackman, and Goldie Hawn and Kurt Russell.

For all its success, Central Park Place was not without problems. Accidents happen, though you always hope they won't happen on your job site. About a year into construction, a thirty-year-old aspiring actor was killed by a wooden post that fell from a high floor. We were deeply saddened—it still upsets me to think of having caused someone's death—and the incident resulted in a delay of several weeks after the city shut down construction to review our procedures and safeguards. That's customary in such cases, but insurance doesn't cover the cost of a shutdown, so a major delay can be expensive. There was one positive result that came out of the accident, however: the city instituted new safety rules for high-rise construction that included the requirement to install safety netting to protect pedestrians from falling building materials. These precautions have no doubt saved many lives over the decades since Central Park Place was built.

The second problem on the project stemmed from the office building we had planned for the SRO site. Because we had already transferred the air rights to the residential tower before permission to demolish came in, the new building couldn't exceed seven stories. (There's also a penthouse, but it's set back from the roof line.) As an added complication, the delay in starting work on the office building meant that Lew Davis wasn't available, so we had to find another architect.

Initially I hired Jack Gordon, who was experienced in commercial design, but almost immediately I was forced to cancel our agreement. Swanke Hayden Connell, a well-known architecture firm that was looking to expand, agreed to lease the new building, but only if they could design it to their specifications. They signed a ten-year lease with a five-year renewal option, taking the top four floors and the penthouse. The second and third floors were leased to smaller companies, including Zagat, publisher of the popular city guides. Retail space on the ground floor was leased to a bank and a food store/restaurant.

Since we weren't tearing down the SRO, we gutted it and merged it with a newly constructed extension to fill out the corner of Eighth Avenue and 58th Street. While the residential tower, completed in 1987, is sleekly modern with its aluminum-and-glass curtain wall, Swanke Hayden Connell's office low-rise uses more traditional steel-frame construction and features large square windows framed in limestone and granite. The office building, completed in 1989, has entrances on both Eighth Avenue and 58th Street; its address is 4 Columbus Circle. The tower address is 301 West 57th Street.

Swanke Hayden Connell seemed like the ideal tenant, but the honeymoon didn't last. Only a few years later, after the recession of the late 1980s brought construction in New York virtually to a halt, the firm was forced to downsize and move out. I had just made a deal to sell the building when I got the news. Legally, I could have gone ahead with the sale, but New York real estate is a small world. I let the buyer go. When Swanke Hayden Connell later defaulted on their rent, Chemical Bank, which had just taken over Manufacturers Hanover, refused to restructure our loan, and we lost the building. Chemical sold 4 Columbus Circle to the office furniture giant Steelcase in 1994. Now known as the Steelcase Building, it still draws attention with its rugged good looks.

At a Crossroads

The Alexandria

Compared to other New York developers, Bill Zeckendorf was very fair and cared about quality. He was a shrewd businessman, but he wanted to build the best building possible. He was a pleasure for Frank Williams to work for and very loyal to Frank.

LAWRENCE ADAMS, architect and former associate in Frank Williams's office

The residential building boom along Broadway on the Upper West Side brought increasing pressure to stand out. The Alexandria, completed in 1991, was notable for its distinctive design and generous apartment size, as well as its prime location. The building sits at the northwest corner of Broadway and West 72nd Street, a busy intersection and transportation hub with a tiny park called Verdi Square.

My partners in the development deal were Peter Malkin, a real estate lawyer who was a part owner of the Empire State

The Alexandria, New York (left)

Sketch of the building by architect Frank Williams

Building, and Arthur Cohen, a well-known real estate investor. We bought the site in 1986 for $21.5 million, intending to hold it until 1988 when the commercial leases in the existing two-story building expired. Tenants at the time included a movie theater, a bank, a shoe store, and an art gallery. Chemical Bank gave us our initial land and construction loan and later a participating mortgage—one that gave them equity—for total financing of $107 million.

Malkin wanted to hire David Childs of Skidmore, Owings & Merrill as the architect, but David had never designed a residential building. I wanted to hire Frank Williams, knowing his genius for laying out apartments. We ended up hiring both, with David handling the overall design and Frank working on the interiors and acting as construction architect. It wasn't the first of my projects they had worked on together: that was Worldwide Plaza, a mixed-use complex on Eighth Avenue in Midtown. My son Will served as project manager for the Alexandria.

As of right, we could build only twenty-two stories, so we transferred air rights from some walk-ups along 72nd Street to add three floors. At the time, most of the new apartment stock on the Upper West Side consisted of studios and one-bedroom apartments. Recognizing how popular with young families the area was becoming, we designed nearly half of the 202 condos with two or more bedrooms. We also gave initial buyers a ten-year tax abatement. We purchased the abatements under a special city program that applied the fees to a low-income housing project on Staten Island.

We named the building the Alexandria as a reference to the loosely Egyptian design motif. With its turreted bay windows, ironwork balconies, colorful palette, and distinctive water tower, the building is a kind of postmodern cousin to more ornate neighbors like the iconic Ansonia one block north. The corner lot made the Alexandria a prime retail location; one of our initial tenants was HMV Records, a British megastore that was just breaking into the U.S. market. I had intended to replace the Embassy Theater with a cinema complex, but I scrapped the plan when I couldn't buy up the entire blockfront along Broadway.

Just as Union Square was a derelict "needle park" when we began work on Zeckendorf Towers in the 1980s, Verdi Square was a well-known drug hangout. We contributed to efforts to clean it up, and it's now an attractive pocket park with benches and planting around a subway entrance.

The Innovator

From the time I started building in the early 1980s, I always had at least two—and usually more—projects on the books. My office expanded along with our workload. In 1984, I hired Terry Soderberg as a project manager. Trained as an architect, Terry was experienced at large-scale development and promptly became an invaluable member of my organization, eventually becoming a senior vice president.

In 1985, I added another superb project manager, Tom Javits. An environmental management major as an undergraduate, Tom had planned to go into some sort of resource management until he went to Harvard Business School, where he was a classmate of my son Will. Tom says he became fascinated with the built environment after hearing a talk I gave at HBS. I'm glad to know I had that effect on him, because he, too, became an excellent project manager and key member of our team, and also rose to senior vice president.

By the time Terry and Tom arrived, my sons were already working for me. Just as I had learned about real estate development from my father, Will and Arthur got firsthand experience from me. From the Columbia on, at least one of my sons was associated with every project in our office. Initially they handled marketing but soon revealed strengths in other areas as well. With his business school background, Will excelled at financing. Arthur had a strong feel for design and laying out interior space.

While we were busy on the Upper West Side, I was also developing properties on the East Side and downtown. As business picked up, we hired help for Marge Fletcher, our office manager, and accountants to keep track of finances. That left me free to do what I liked best and did best: put together deals.

For me, the thrill of developing was not in watching a building go up: I seldom spent any time on job sites, leaving construction supervision to my project managers. My passion was putting together the deal. I loved every aspect of it: finding a property, assembling a site, securing financing, hiring an architect, and working on the plans. Once we broke ground, I was happy to turn over day-to-day supervision, only stepping back in if a problem arose or we needed more financing.

The project managers had their hands full. At any given time, the office was juggling multiple projects, at various stages of completion. I might be putting together financing for a couple of projects and finalizing plans for others, while some of our buildings were under construction and still others were being marketed. Terry remembers days when we had meetings for several projects going on simultaneously in different rooms in the office, and we had to run back and forth between them.

While all this was happening, I would be scouting properties and considering half a dozen or so potential projects. Some would go forward; others wouldn't pan out. I was always on the lookout for the next big thing. Sometimes I would spot a site while driving around New York, or I might track a parcel for years, waiting for an opportunity to buy. Other times I would hear about a property from a broker or an investor or another developer. Real estate brokers like Bob Shapiro and Ed Lewis brought me properties because they knew I would offer a fair price.

A Noble Experiment

Delmonico Plaza

Bill decided to move his office to Delmonico Plaza and asked me to design the interior. It was the mid-1980s, and postmodernism was rampant. But Bill had a lot of modernist furniture, including a desk that I.M. Pei had designed for his father. There was a lot of talk about what we should do with the furniture; it wasn't in style at the time. Then we decided: we're keeping this furniture. It was a bold move on Bill's part that he elected to keep it. We took his father's desk and had a new glass top made for it.

BIRCH COFFEY, interior architect

My first ground-up project on the East Side was Delmonico Plaza, a $105 million office condominium at 55 East 59th Street, just around the corner from the Hotel Delmonico, where our office and my apartment were located. I started buying the property piece by piece in the late 1970s and early 1980s. I picked up a Gristedes supermarket that was very inexpensive, as well

Rendering of Delmonico Plaza

View of Delmonico Plaza, New York, from 59th Street (opposite)

as three or four tenement buildings. I also bought air rights to a six-story building that belonged to the French Institute Alliance Française. My plan was to build an office tower midblock. Zoning regulations limited the height of midblock buildings, but with the air rights I could go up twenty-four floors, for a total of 270,000 square feet of office space, with retail on the street level.

Lew Davis of Davis, Brody was the architect. This was one of a number of projects I worked on with Lew, including Zeckendorf Towers, the Copley, and Central Park Place. Like all of Lew's buildings, Delmonico Plaza is striking, with alternating horizontal bands of slate and granite on the facade. As part of our agreement with the French Institute, we built them a new concert/lecture hall on the ground floor.

Birch Coffey designed the interiors of the building, including our office. Hack Wilson was again my equity partner, and his son Cary was the project manager.

Delmonico Plaza was the first office tower in Midtown Manhattan built specifically as a condominium. (Other office condos at the time were conversions.) Most developers like to hold on to commercial buildings, leasing out the office space as an ongoing source of income. However, I didn't want to be a landlord any more than I wanted to be a hotelier and preferred the business model of our residential condos: sell off the individual units as quickly as possible and get out.

Larry Silverstein, a New York developer who later was one of my partners on the Ronald Reagan Building and International Trade Center in Washington, D.C., called Delmonico Plaza a "bellwether." If the condo concept was successful, he said, it would be a game-changer in commercial development. Unfortunately, that didn't happen. Although our analyses showed what companies could save by buying rather than leasing offices, sales were sluggish. Some of that might have been the timing: the commercial building boom of the 1980s had flooded the market with new offices. What was more significant, however, is that the business model didn't work for most

companies: they were reluctant to tie up capital in office space, worried it would limit their flexibility if changing market conditions required them to contract.

We were among the first occupants of Delmonico Plaza when it opened in early 1986. We had outgrown our office in the Hotel Delmonico, and it was a relief to move into a full floor in the new building. But the building was losing money, so I ended up selling out, then renting back our office space until 1992, when I closed down my operations in New York.

Selling Convenience

The Cosmopolitan and the Vanderbilt

At any one time in our office we probably had two or three projects in construction, two or three completed that we were marketing, two or three assemblages we were working on, and probably a dozen ideas for new projects. That's what Bill was always working on: the next wave. What are the new ideas? What are the opportunities? He still has any number of things on the drawing board that were never realized.

TOM JAVITS, former senior VP and managing director, Zeckendorf Company

We built two apartment high-rises, the Cosmopolitan and the Vanderbilt, in the heart of the Midtown East business district. Both opened in 1986 and emphasized amenities and convenience.

The Cosmopolitan, on East 48th Street between Lexington and Third Avenues, is a thirty-five-story condominium that was among the first residential buildings in the city to offer

The Cosmopolitan, New York (left)

The Vanderbilt, New York

concierge services like maids, valets, and phones set up for business. Given those conveniences and the strategic location—steps from Grand Central Station, the United Nations, and corporate headquarters along Madison and Park Avenues—the 207-unit high-rise was tailor-made for buyers looking for a pied-à-terre.

A decade earlier, Tishman Realty & Construction, which became the mega-developer Tishman Speyer in 1978, had tried to develop the whole block as a new headquarters for the New York Telephone Company. Unable to empty out an old hotel on the site, they abandoned the plan, and the land reverted to the owner, Sol Goldman. We bought the property from Goldman, a real estate investor who at one time was the city's largest landlord. (I once told a *New York Times* reporter that Goldman "buys property the way other people buy common stock.")

By the time we bought the site, it was a 13,000-square-foot parking lot, so we had no building to tear down or tenants to relocate. We acquired air rights from a small apartment building east of the property and hired an award-winning architecture firm, Gruzen Samton Steinglass. The building they designed, with its rosy brick cladding and vertical columns of bay windows, was a critical success. The lobby was designed by Valerian Rybar, noted for his opulent interiors for upper-crust clients with names like Rothschild, Newhouse, Schlumberger, Onassis, and Niarchos. My partner in the $50 million project was Transcon, headed by Harshad Shah, an Indian investor.

Most of the units—studios and one-bedrooms—went to corporate buyers or investors planning to rent them out. In fact, six months in, only 15 of the first 131 apartments had sold as primary residences. An on-site agent handled rentals at no charge. Bankers Trust bought two floors in the building for housing visiting employees and, at our suggestion, hired Brown Harris Stevens to manage the apartments.

The second project, the Vanderbilt, sits between Second and Third Avenues on East 40th Street. With 41 stories and 369 apartments, it is larger than the Cosmopolitan and, with its corner balconies and stepped profile, more dramatic in design. Frank Williams was our architect.

My partners in this $75 million project were World Wide Holdings and Colonial Equity, and here, too, we were appealing to a corporate buyer. Proximity to Grand Central Station, the United Nations, university clubs, and Midtown office buildings was a major selling point. With apartment sizes ranging from studios to two-bedrooms, the Vanderbilt was aimed at younger buyers. To attract this market, we put in a state-of-the-art health club with a swimming pool, sauna, and basketball and squash courts. In-building access to the underground garage appealed to the security-conscious.

Breaking New Ground

The Belaire

The Belaire was another financial home run.

ARTHUR ZECKENDORF

Building apartments near a hospital center is good for business: doctors welcome the convenience, and buyers find it reassuring to have top-flight medical care close at hand. One of the most unusual deals of my career was one we struck with the Hospital for Special Surgery, a world-famous orthopedic and rehabilitation facility on Manhattan's Upper East Side. The result of our partnership was the Belaire, a mixed-use project combining condominiums, offices, and hospital housing.

In 1986, Donald Broas, executive director of HSS, contacted me through a broker. The hospital had outgrown its building on East 70th Street and needed additional space. At the same time, it was sitting on an underutilized property nearby that it wanted to develop for offices and staff housing. Would we be interested?

You bet. The site was a piece of prime real estate—a through-block site from East 71st Street to 72nd Street between York Avenue and the East River. The only structure on the plot was the hospital's five-story parking garage. The deal we struck was highly advantageous to both HSS and us. We would pay the hospital $20 million for the garage and its air rights and build an apartment tower on the site. In exchange, HSS would pay construction costs for us to build them a new facility, along with an underground garage. As far as we knew, this novel arrangement was a first for any hospital or developer.

Rendering of the Belaire

The trick was to fit all this on the same site. Architecturally it was quite a challenge. Frank Williams rose to the occasion with an ingenious solution: "two buildings stacked vertically," as he described it. We built one high-rise building, devoting the first fourteen floors to HSS, with an entrance on 71st Street. Then the twenty-five floors above that contain 147 luxury condos, with a separate entrance and lobby on 72nd Street. The underground garage has separate access for both. Frank designed the overall building, laid out the residential interiors, and drew up the construction plans. Ulrich Franzen, a well-known New York architect experienced in health care facilities, was hired by the hospital to plan the interiors of their floors.

Kumagai Gumi's KG Land division was again our financial partner. Just as at Central Park Place, they wanted a credit for their balance sheet. This time, however, they also insisted on being a construction company of record. So on paper the Belaire was a joint venture of KG and Turner Construction, although Turner did all the work. Turner specialized in commercial construction; the Belaire was their first apartment house.

The project started off smoothly. Air quality is a major concern when building near a medical facility: hospitals incinerate medical waste. One of the first things we did was conduct extensive testing to make sure emissions from the smokestacks at the nearby New York–Cornell Hospital complex were well within EPA limits. We secured all the necessary building permits and did our preliminary geotechnical report on the soil, rock, and water

Tom Javits, Zeckendorf Company project manager for the Belaire

conditions at the site. We demolished the existing garage without incident and began digging the hole for our foundation and the underground garage.

We were three or four months into the job, with a hole about thirty feet deep, when Tom Javits called me from the site to say that the buildings department had put a stop order on our site because of a problem with the foundation of the building next door. A problem? That was an understatement, it turns out.

The construction superintendent had called Tom, expressing the urgency of the matter in more pungent terms: "Javits, you'd better get your butt down here. The engineer on site has stopped the digging because the building to the west of us is in danger of falling into our hole."

Tom rushed to the site and met with the Turner engineers. It turned out that when the eighteen-story apartment house next door to our site went up in the 1960s, it wasn't built to code. Instead of resting on proper foundations, it was sitting on mud. It had been leaning against the garage foundations on our site for support, and when we tore down the garage, there went the support. The building was on the verge of tumbling into our hole.

None of this was our fault: we'd done everything by the book, making sure we properly shored up the abutting buildings as we dug. But when cracks appeared under the neighboring building, our engineers had no choice but to shut us down.

It didn't matter that the fault lay next door. We had to take care of the problem. We weren't allowed to proceed until we had put in a new foundation for the neighboring building and modified our own foundation. That added months to the job. Normally we would have been in and out of the hole in six months. Instead, it took us ten, jeopardizing our commitment to the hospital to finish their space by a certain date.

Meanwhile, fixing the foundations cost us a lot of money as well as time. We had to pay the workers for an extra four months as well as service our loan: we had borrowed more than $75 million from Chase to buy the land and fund construction on the residential portion of the building. HSS was in a better position. Shrewdly, they had invested the $20 million we paid for their land, pledging it as collateral against $20 million in low-interest tax-exempt bonds from the New York State Dormitory Authority. This allowed them to benefit from the difference between the yield on their investment and the interest rate on the bonds. Out of the proceeds, they were paying us monthly for their portion of the construction costs.

Unfortunately, the foundation wasn't the end of our problems. Midway through construction, our electrical contractor went bankrupt. We had gotten a construction bond against just such a disruption and were successful in forcing the bonding company to reduce our costs, since the issue was caused by the subcontractor's breach of contract. But this led to yet another delay and claims by other subcontractors.

Sketch of the Belaire by architect Frank Williams

To our relief, in the end the building was a great success. The hospital was pleased with its space, which is entered through a spacious courtyard with landscaping and a fountain. The HSS facility includes offices and apartments. Originally built to be staff housing, the apartments are now rented out to hospital patients and visitors.

Our apartment tower, with its red brick facade, setback penthouse floors, and distinctive window treatment, was well received by critics as well as upscale buyers. The location of the building—on a cul-de-sac at the end of East 72nd Street, overlooking the East River—also appealed to our clientele.

Birch Coffey, who did the interiors for Delmonico Plaza and Central Park Place, designed the public spaces of the Belaire, including the lobby, corridors, workout space, swimming pool, and sales office. The lobby was a particular challenge: it's a long, narrow room with a twenty-five-foot ceiling. Birch used horizontal bands of wood on the walls to bring the space into balance. In the 1980s, apartment house lobbies were starting to become smaller and less grand. But we gave Birch free rein to use luxurious materials and stylish furniture—this was a high-end condo, after all. He did the lobby floors in marble and the ceiling in gold leaf with indirect lighting.

Here, as at Central Park Place, we planned the apartment layouts so that adjacent units could be readily combined. Though we pioneered this strategy, it was soon widely copied by other developers. At the Belaire, the approach was a particularly effective marketing tool: Marvin Traub, chairman of Bloomingdale's, was among the first to buy two units to combine.

My son Arthur moved into the Belaire when it opened in 1988 and was living there in 2006 when a small plane carrying New York Yankees pitcher Cory Lidle and his flight instructor crashed into the side of the building. Fire gutted two of the apartments, and smoke forced residents, including the author Carol Higgins Clark, to evacuate. The building shook but stood firm. When Frank Williams, along with the engineers and buildings department, showed up to assess the situation, they found no structural damage. Frank wasn't surprised. He had designed the Belaire with reinforced concrete—so it could withstand a kitchen explosion, he said. None of us had factored in a plane crash, though.

View of the Belaire, New York, from Roosevelt Island (opposite)

Two other residential projects on the Upper East Side presented interesting challenges, though nothing like what was involved at the Belaire. I had a minor position in Park Avenue Court, a condominium completed in 1989 that was a gut renovation and conversion of the old Gimbels East department store on Lexington Avenue between East 86th and 87th Streets. The original building—designed by Abbott, Merkt & Company, a construction firm that specialized in industrial plants and department stores—was only fourteen years old in 1986 when Gimbels decided to close its uptown branch. Developer Larry Silverstein and Melvin Simon, one of the largest shopping mall operators in the United States, decided to convert the store into apartments.

At first glance, the windowless twelve-story structure was an unlikely candidate for a residential conversion. But it was structurally sound, and our architect, David Childs of Skidmore, Owings & Merrill, turned it into a seventeen-story residence

Park Avenue Court, New York (left)

The Gotham, New York

with oversized windows. He carved a courtyard out of the center of the building, completely rebuilt the top floors into two towers, and faced the exterior in red brick, recalling the prewar apartment houses along Park Avenue, a block to the west. The limestone base was reconfigured for retail, including a Barnes & Noble that has since moved. The big-box stores Best Buy, Petco, and Staples now occupy the commercial space.

When it came to marketing the 223 condos, the loftlike, thirteen-foot ceilings—unusually high for Manhattan apartments—were a draw, and architecture critics cited the impressive entrance on 87th Street. But despite the attractive design and high-end amenities, which included a swimming pool and a yoga/Pilates studio, sales were sluggish. Financially, the project was a disaster. I sold my share in the early 1990s as I was trying to restructure my debt.

My last condominium on the Upper East Side, the Gotham, was another collaboration with Frank Williams. A twenty-seven-story mixed-use tower at the corner of East 87th Street and Third Avenue, the $150 million project included 241 apartments and 10,000 square feet of retail. We tore down a movie theater on the site, then built a Loews theater complex into the ground floor and basement of the new building. The building is handsome with many attractive features, including balconies and terraces and split-levels in many of the apartments. But when the Gotham opened in 1991 sales were slow and most of the apartments ended up as rentals.

The Gotham was among the properties I lost to my creditors. Some years later, my sons bought the building from the bank in a foreclosure auction.

Downtown

The Hudson Residences

Bill was the quintessential urban pioneer. He pushed Manhattan's boundaries in every direction.

HERB STURZ, former chair, New York City planning commission

Early in my career, I established a reputation for taking on challenging properties and opening up new neighborhoods. Lower Manhattan wasn't yet a hot residential area in the mid-1980s when I built a trio of apartment houses in Battery Park City, a new development near the southern tip of Manhattan.

Located on the far West Side, along the Hudson River, Battery Park City is a quiet enclave just minutes from Wall Street and steps from Brookfield Place, formerly the World Financial Center. The prime location wasn't so advantageous on 9/11, however, when the neighborhood suffered the fallout—literally—of the collapsing Twin Towers. Hudson View East, the building closest to the World Trade Center site, was damaged by falling airplane parts. There are haunting photos of Battery Park City

Hudson Tower, Battery Park City, New York (left)

Site plan of Battery Park City showing the three Hudson Residences

apartments abandoned when the residents fled, the contents in some cases, the remnants of breakfast—blanketed in white ash like a modern-day Pompeii.

Pre-9/11, the area was about to take off. Built on landfill—including rock and soil excavated during the construction of the World Trade Center and sand dredged from Ambrose Channel, the main shipping lane in and out of New York Harbor—Battery Park City is one of the largest planned communities in the United States, and easily one of the most attractivc. Half of its ninety-two acres are devoted to parks and public space, and all the apartments are within a block of the waterfront.

Battery Park City is a partnership between an authority set up by the state's Urban Development Corporation and selected private developers. Originally, six developers were named to develop the main sites, and minor sites were parceled out to others. Three of the sites were earmarked for the Hudson Residences. They're just south of the former World Financial Center, which was under construction at approximately the same time. With a total of 350 apartments in three separate buildings, the Hudson Residences were the first condominiums to go up in Battery Park City.

Jason Carter, a tennis pro turned real estate developer, asked us to help him develop one of the buildings, Hudson Tower, which opened in 1986. A Davis, Brody design with 134 apartments on sixteen floors, the building sold out in ten days. My son Will was heavily involved in developing Hudson Tower, as well as two other condominiums in the complex, Hudson View West and Hudson View East. We were asked to come in on those properties after the original developers couldn't finance them alone.

Hudson View West, a midrise condo with nine floors and 107 apartments that was designed by Conklin & Rossant, opened in 1985. Hudson View East, a nineteen-floor condo with 109 residential units that was designed by Mitchell/Giurgola, opened the following year.

Hudson Tower sits on the 1.2-mile esplanade along the river and has panoramic views of the Statue of Liberty and the New Jersey skyline. Hudson View West and East, though slightly inland, also offer ready access to the riverfront and green space.

Design guidelines for Battery Park City were strict. The planners wanted to create a neighborhood that referenced the best in classic New York residential architecture. All three of our buildings have the requisite limestone base, red brick cladding, and finely detailed facade.

The Transformer

Business was good. In the mid-1980s, we were the most active developers in New York, and by the end of the decade, we had completed some seventeen ground-up projects, with more in the works. Our projects were selling well, and they had won us a reputation for well-designed, well-built buildings that improved the neighborhoods around them. Banks were eager to lend to us, and we could count on major investors like the Japanese construction giant Kumagai Gumi to come in as equity partners.

As I became known for tackling difficult sites and successfully venturing into risky areas, opportunities opened up on a grander scale. Brokers were bringing me bigger and better properties, the deals were getting more complex, and I had the confidence to plunge into larger projects that ventured into unknown territory. No longer content just to improve a building's immediate surroundings, I was opening up neglected parts of the city and transforming whole communities.

Big projects take more time and money and involve more parties. All of that ups the ante. In executing the four biggest projects of my career, I discovered the many ways a project could go right—or horribly wrong.

Revitalizing Union Square

Zeckendorf Towers

Someone had to go first, take a chance, and provide a strong foundation that others could build on to turn around a neighborhood that suffered from dilapidated buildings and as a hangout for drug dealers. In 1984, Bill Zeckendorf stepped forward with the ambitious and challenging plan for Zeckendorf Towers, dedicated to his father. This project stirred hope, brought excitement, added optimism, and was a critical vote of confidence for the neighborhood.

WILLIAM HAINES, president of the Lower Fifth Avenue Association

The first of the large transformative projects I undertook was a one-million-square-foot mixed-use complex covering the entire block from the east side of Union Square to Irving Place, between East 14th and 15th Streets. I named it Zeckendorf Towers in honor of my father and his accomplishments, not as a billboard for myself. As it happened, both of my sons worked

Bill Zeckendorf with his sons, Will and Arthur, in front of a model of Zeckendorf Towers

View of Zeckendorf Towers, New York, from across Union Square (opposite)

on the project, so in a sense, all three generations of the family were involved.

As Manhattan's second busiest transportation hub and the gateway to downtown, Union Square was ideal for a large-scale development. What wasn't ideal back in the 1970s and early 1980s was the park at the center of the square. A high-crime haven for junkies and derelicts known as "needle park," it had a spillover effect on the area around it.

It hadn't always been that way. Laid out in the 1830s, Union Square soon was home to many of New York's wealthiest residents, whose elegant town houses surrounded the fenced-in

Vintage photograph of S. Klein buildings along Park Avenue between East 14th and 15th Streets

green. With the arrival of the Academy of Music in the 1850s, the area became the city's theater district. After the Civil War, Union Square was a key point on "Ladies' Mile," a string of fashionable shops stretching from East 8th Street to 23rd Street. When the shops and theaters moved uptown at the beginning of the twentieth century, the square became a gathering place for political rallies and soapbox orators. As immigrants and workers moved into the area, shops selling bargain merchandise followed. After World War II, Union Square went into free fall, and by the 1970s it was a thriving marketplace for drug deals.

For decades, the retail giant on Union Square was S. Klein. The flagship of a famous discount chain, it opened in the early twentieth century. With 300,000 square feet of space spread over eleven small, nineteenth-century buildings, S. Klein occupied the entire block at the southeastern corner of the square, where Park Avenue meets East 14th Street. By the 1970s, S. Klein was owned by the Rapid-American Corporation, a holding company run by the corporate raider Meshulam Riklis. Riklis had built a financial empire through leveraged buyouts of retail chains and numerous other businesses. He closed the S. Klein store in 1975, and as the years went on, the derelict buildings became a visible symbol of Union Square's decline.

Though I was busy with other projects at the time, I kept a close eye on the S. Klein site. At one and three-quarters acres, it was large enough to build something substantial that could relieve the blight in Union Square and start transformation of the neighborhood around it. The property was the key to unlocking Lower Manhattan from Park Avenue South on down. I wasn't the only one who saw its potential. An Argentinian retailer briefly floated plans to refurbish and reopen the S. Klein store. And Riklis himself made enough noise about erecting a forty-story tower on the lot to draw strong opposition from the community. Other developers looked at the site but were put off by the dicey neighborhood.

I saw my chance. I tried to arrange a meeting with Riklis but was unsuccessful, only getting through to him when our mutual friend Justin Colin interceded. The meeting went nowhere: Riklis didn't want to sell. Still, over the next few years I patiently but persistently conveyed my interest. Then in the summer of 1983, Riklis's sons-in-law, Elie Hirschfeld and Irwin Ackerman, came to me with an offer: if I could put together a development deal, I could have the property. Their price for bringing it to me was 50 percent carried interest—half the profits on whatever I developed, with no investment on their part. And I would have to pay Riklis for the land, of course. I wasn't thrilled with the terms, but I knew it was the only way to get the site.

I couldn't help but recall the veiled threat that Elie Hirschfeld's father, Abraham, had made when I balked at extending his payment schedule for the Statler Hotel. There was none of that here, however. Elie Hirschfeld gave me a generous two years to put together a development deal: arrange financing, secure design plans, line up commercial tenants, and get the community on board.

Area residents had been lobbying city and local officials for years to clean up Union Square and revitalize the neighborhood. The Parks Department had already launched a project to drive out the drug dealers and reclaim the park, and the Metropolitan Transportation Authority had started sprucing up the subway station. The City Planning Commission had proposed guidelines that would permit greater density in the area and offer a bonus to any developer who made further improvements to the subway and park.

Architects Sam Brody and Lew Davis holding a photomontage of Zeckendorf Towers, with the Con Edison building in the background

With the new zoning, we would be able to build a one-million-square-foot structure with a four-hundred-car underground garage. I thought the best use of the site would be a single building containing both commercial and residential space. I had a better feel for residential than for offices and retail, but under the new zoning the project had to be mixed-use, so we were limited in the amount of residential we could build.

I knew that aesthetics would play a key role in selling the project to the community, so I enlisted Lew Davis of Davis, Brody. Lew had received acclaim for his Waterside Plaza and Riverbend complexes, and he had already designed a couple of buildings for us. Our community-liaison expert, Edith Fisher, began working her magic with local residents and business interests. Anxious to see the area improve, most were optimistic about our plans. One gesture we made right away was to give the nonprofit Vineyard Theatre 9,000 square feet on the lower level and ground floor of our new building for a 197-seat performance space; the group would pay a token rent of $1 a year in perpetuity. We were giving up prime retail space and the annual revenue from leasing it, but I figured it was a worthy sacrifice to build community goodwill.

Even with Edith's deft handling, however, we almost didn't get local approval. I'll never forget our first meeting with the planning boards. I say "boards"—plural—because our central location meant that representatives of four different community boards would have a say, along with a fifth representative whose job it was to coordinate the other four. The conference room in the Davis, Brody office was jammed. Edith outlined the potential benefits to the neighborhood, including the theater, the refurbished subway station, and the supermarket we planned to install on the building's ground floor. Then Lew brought out a model of his proposed design: a seven-story commercial base with retail on the ground floor and a single, immense residential tower rising from the center.

The reaction was terrible. The outcry was so loud it probably reached our office fifty blocks uptown. Lew's tower would dwarf everything else in the square, the community reps squawked, and it would block sunlight everywhere around it. Furthermore, it would cut off views of the Con Edison building with its iconic clock tower, a neighborhood landmark. We were in trouble—and I had no idea what to do. Then Lew, a savvy diplomat as well as a great designer, stepped in and told the group he had another idea. He removed the tower from the model and broke it into four pieces, then carefully placed them at each corner. Now the building consisted of four twenty-story towers rising from the seven-story base. To this day, I don't know if Lew's demonstration was preplanned or a last-minute stroke of genius.

While I was waiting for Riklis to close the sale, I lined up a construction loan from Citibank. I had planned to bring in Kumagai Gumi. But this was going to be a $225 million project—larger and more expensive than any of our previous projects together. After I made several trips to Japan, they agreed to participate.

Then I had to find commercial tenants. Having developed a good relationship with A&P at the Copley, I got them to take 22,000 square feet—most of the ground floor—for what would be their largest supermarket in New York. There was no other grocery store of size nearby, and the famous Union Square Greenmarket was just getting started. The supermarket would be a draw in selling the apartments, as would the fitness center and swimming pool we had planned for the top floor of the commercial base.

That left us with 300,000 square feet of office space to fill. Lew Davis designed the corporate floors to wrap around an atrium open to the sky, which limited how the space could be divided. But at the price we'd set—$20 a square foot—nothing comparable was available, so we didn't think leasing would pose a problem. Through the broker John Cushman we struck a deal with a major publishing house to take all the office space. There was just one condition: they had to be able to move in before their current lease expired. Unfortunately, our construction took longer than expected, and when it was clear we wouldn't be able to meet their deadline, the publisher pulled out.

It was a slow time for office rentals, and since our space was unusual, I knew it wouldn't be easy to find another tenant. But we couldn't afford to let 300,000 square feet sit empty. Finally, I got a call from a broker whose client, Integrated Resources, a financial services firm, wanted the space. We did our due diligence, and everything seemed to be in order. Then we started hearing rumors that the owners of the company were selling off stock. The broker assured us that the company was sound: the owners were just diversifying. We needed the tenant, so we went ahead with the deal. The broker was a tough negotiator:

Arthur, Will, and Bill Zeckendorf reviewing plans for Zeckendorf Towers

Integrated threatened to pull out unless we agreed to six months' free rent and a generous $20-a-square-foot work letter for renovations. (A work letter spells out what the landlord will do in building out a tenant's office space.) The terms weren't ideal, but at least we had a firm commitment and a twenty-five-year lease.

We finished construction in 1987. Integrated Resources moved into their new space and then, a week before the first rent check was due, filed for bankruptcy. We hadn't even paid the broker's fee: that was to come out of Integrated Resource's first rent payment. Kumagai Gumi, anxious to avoid a legal fight over the fee, advanced us $5 million to pay off the broker.

Our initial plan had been to sell the office portion of the complex as soon as the building opened. Then we decided to hang onto it for the income. But losing our tenant meant we were unable to pay Citibank the interest on our loan. I got our lender, Equitable Life, to take over the payments on the office portion of the loan and surrendered the office space to them. We arranged to continue overseeing the leasing and management of the offices and retail. After Integrated Resources left, we converted the office to multitenant occupancy and leased space to several businesses, including the Macmillan/McGraw-Hill School Publishing Company and HIP, a health insurance

Zeckendorf Towers cupolas at night

provider. Eventually the entire office unit was sold to Beth Israel Hospital for its outpatient services. Beth Israel is still there today.

We had less trouble selling the residential portion of the complex. My sons came up with a clever marketing campaign. They divided the 672 condos into four different "neighborhoods," corresponding to the four towers, and gave each one a different name. The condos were sold out in eighteen months. My aim had been to offer affordable residences in an architectural setting that was sensitive to the existing community. If the sales figures are any indication, we succeeded.

Every deal has its stories. Zeckendorf Towers is no exception. The building fills the entire block, which meant razing every existing structure on the lot. Invariably, in such cases there's a holdout. For us, it was an elderly man who for years had owned a small newsstand/cigar shop on East 14th Street. Finally, at the eleventh hour, he agreed to sell. Terry Soderberg, who was our project manager at the time, remembers that sale:

> The owner held out for $150,000—a huge amount back then. He also demanded to be paid in cash, so the closing took

place in a Citibank vault. There were stacks of money piled on the table, and the seller sat there and counted every bill, then stuffed the cash into a canvas bag. We took him outside the bank, said goodbye, and told him, "You're on your own." He got into a car and headed for JFK. It's a customs violation to take more than $10,000 out of the country without notifying thc authorities in advance, and odds are the money will be seized. We never heard what happened when our seller got to the airport.

I'm very proud of Zeckendorf Towers. I'm prejudiced, of course, but I think it's one of the most beautiful complexes in the city. When the pyramidal cupolas on the four residential towers are lit up at night, the sight is magnificent.

My greatest source of pride, however, is the impact Zeckendorf Towers had on Union Square. Land values rose 50 percent after the building went up and have continued to climb. It is widely credited with being the most important factor in the revitalization of the area, the catalyst for its redevelopment. No sooner had we broken ground in 1984 than other developers started building around us. Restaurateur Danny Meyer broke new ground of another sort when he opened one of the country's most acclaimed restaurants, Union Square Cafe, just off the square. Even as Terry Soderberg had to shoo the homeless out of the doorways every morning, the area continued to improve. Today trendy Union Square is a bustling center of downtown life—one of the city's most desirable places to live, work, and play.

In 1996, the 14th Street–Union Square Local Development Corporation honored several of us for our part in the rebirth of the area. William Haines, president of the Lower Fifth Avenue Association, called me a "true visionary" who "went the extra mile in consulting with and responding to the concerns of the community." I firmly believe that cultivating good relationships with local residents and businesses is essential for transforming neighborhoods. That's another important lesson I learned from my father.

Opening Up Eighth Avenue

Worldwide Plaza

Worldwide Plaza was the right thing in the right place. It has all these great sweeping views because nothing will ever be built up around it. And it has presence. If you look at the local TV news programs at night, half of them have helicopters flying around this building, because it's a symbol. It's unique.

DAVID CHILDS, partner, Skidmore, Owings & Merrill

Somebody once asked me what inspired Worldwide Plaza. "Four acres," I said. A four-acre empty lot in Midtown Manhattan was unheard of in the 1980s, and it couldn't help but get my imagination going.

Worldwide Plaza was my biggest and most complicated project in New York—a sprawling multiuse complex comprising a forty-nine-story office tower with 1.5 million square feet of office space, a thirty-nine-story apartment building, a cluster of townhouse condos, retail, a health club, a multiscreen movie theater, a landscaped public plaza, a five-hundred-car underground parking

Old Madison Square Garden on the site later occupied by Worldwide Plaza

garage, and a new subway station—all packed onto one giant lot. Building Worldwide Plaza, which opened in 1989, took four and a half years, $545 million from a consortium of fifteen banks, and a gargantuan crew of architects, engineers, project and construction managers, contractors, subcontractors, and workers from more than forty trades. There could be a book devoted to this project, and indeed there was. Karl Sabbagh's *Skyscraper: The Making of a Building* was the companion to a five-part television series that aired on PBS in 1990.

Located in a section of Manhattan known as Hell's Kitchen—or more euphemistically, Clinton—Worldwide Plaza stands on the block between Eighth and Ninth Avenues, from West 49th to 50th Street. From 1925 until 1968, the site was occupied by the third Madison Square Garden. (Among standout events at MSG III were the first pro basketball game and two appearances by Marilyn Monroe. At one she rode an elephant at a party hosted by Elizabeth Taylor and Mike Todd; at the other she sang "Happy Birthday" to President John F. Kennedy at an event in his honor.) After the Garden moved to its present location above Penn Station, the old building was torn down, and the site sat empty for seventeen years. Hell's Kitchen was the seamy underbelly of the city, overrun with prostitutes, drug dealers, and addicts who roamed Eighth Avenue, with its porn theaters, peep shows, SROs, and gritty bars. Still, it was the biggest vacant lot in Manhattan, and every developer had considered it. In the 1970s, Victor Elmaleh, my frequent equity partner, had tried to put up an amusement park on the property. Gulf & Western, which owned the land, would periodically announce plans to build a new headquarters on the site, only to scrap the idea when the neighborhood protested.

So the property remained the city's largest open-air parking lot until 1984, when Gulf & Western finally decided to put it on the block. The response was underwhelming. Eighth Avenue was such a mess that most developers figured no respectable commercial tenant would consider moving there. But I'd had my eye on the site since my days at Webb & Knapp. Beyond the grit and grime and obvious drawbacks, I saw a choice opportunity to open up Midtown West. In building my way down Broadway, I'd gotten as far as Columbus Circle and West 57th Street, and here was a chance to pioneer yet another undeveloped area. Times Square was girding up for a renewal; a major development seven blocks north would not only clean up a ravaged area but also be a catalyst for transforming a broad swath of the West Side.

I put in a bid.

By the time the bidding reached $70 million, only two of us remained. Bidding against me was Mort Zuckerman, a Canadian making inroads in real estate and media investment. I won the site for $100 million. Not cheap, given the location. But we had run the numbers, and our projections told us we could go that high.

Looking back, I realize how optimistic we were at the start. For any project, you factor in the cost of construction delays and overruns, and the extra interest on your loans that results. But Worldwide Plaza was unlike anything built in New York in decades, if ever, and it had a set of expectations and headaches all its own. Some of them were pretty dramatic.

Once we acquired the property, we had to decide what to do with it. To justify the purchase price, we would have to build something big, and to make the greatest impact, it would have to be mixed-use. The site was way too big for a single structure, so I envisioned a complex like Rockefeller Center, with a large office component and a separate, smaller residential component.

Mort wanted in on the deal, but I already had a team of equity investors I'd been working with: Victor Elmaleh and Frank Stanton of World Wide Holdings; Arthur Cohen; and KG Land, Kumagai Gumi's New York subsidiary. Ordinarily that group would have been enough equity to secure a loan, but this was too big a project for Manufacturers Hanover, our banker in the past, and other banks weren't eager to take on so much risk in a marginal location. Finally, the real estate advisors Sonnenblick-Goldman put us together with the Canadian Imperial Bank of Commerce. Joined by Manufacturers Hanover, Canadian Imperial led an international consortium that agreed to lend us $545 million for land purchase and construction. The terms were stiff, however, and we had to make personal guarantees on the loan. I always tried to avoid personal guarantees: if you put up personal assets as collateral and the project runs into trouble, you risk losing your assets.

No sooner had we signed the loan agreement than we got a piece of good news. The advertising giant Ogilvy & Mather Worldwide had been talking with Mort Zuckerman about leasing space if he built on the site, and now they were eager to talk to us. Our plans called for 1.5 million square feet of office space. Ogilvy & Mather wanted close to 600,000 square feet—40 percent of the building. They were prepared to pay $100 million for the space in exchange for 17 percent equity and an option to expand.

This was the start we needed. It would put the project on a more stable financial footing, making us more attractive to the banks. Plus, leasing so early, and to such a strong tenant, would give other potential tenants confidence in us and allay concerns about the location. Office towers were springing up along Broadway, but the fact that one of the world's largest and most respected ad agencies was choosing to move its headquarters to Eighth Avenue sent a positive message to the entire New York

business community about the viability of our building and the far edge of Midtown West.

Ogilvy took a long-term lease, starting at $20 a square foot and rising $1 a year—a bargain even in our untried location. We also gave them a generous allowance of $20 a square foot for building out the space. Signing on while we were still in the planning stage gave them another advantage: they would have considerable say in the design of their own space and could also weigh in on plans for the building as a whole. We had tentatively sketched out two office towers, but Ogilvy & Mather wanted so much contiguous space that we decided on a single tower with floors as large as 40,000 square feet.

It was essential to pick the right architect for the project. For the office tower, my first thought was Lew Davis. But Lew and Victor Elmaleh couldn't stand one another, so I asked Terry Soderberg, who had trained as an architect, to draw up a list of alternatives. There were three firms on his list: Kohn Pedersen Fox, Cesar Pelli & Associates, and Skidmore, Owings & Merrill. A few years earlier, while working on a project in Washington, D.C., that hadn't panned out, I had gotten to know David Childs, an SOM partner then based in the capital, who had recently become the senior design partner in SOM's New York office. Childs had no experience with skyscrapers, but he was smart and imaginative and had a large firm behind him that could manage every aspect of a project as big and complicated as ours. Plus, I felt I kind of owed him for all the work he had done on spec on my Washington project.

Worldwide Plaza, New York (opposite)

Today, architects have to jump through hoops to land a commission, entering design competitions and submitting detailed plans. Back in the 1980s, the selection process was far more intuitive. We asked the three firms we were considering to come to our office. Childs, accompanied by Leon Moed, SOM's partner in charge of business, had the second appointment on the first day. I described the site and what we wanted to do with it. SOM needed a big commission at that point, and their financial proposal was almost too good: $5 a square foot in design fees. That would come

David Childs, architect of the Worldwide Plaza office tower

to about $7.5 million, including all consultants' fees, for the office tower. The next day, after we'd interviewed all three firms, I asked Terry, "What do you think?" "It's obvious" was his reply. It was to me, too. I went back to my office and consulted with my other partners, then phoned David Childs and said, "It's yours."

Childs decided to position the office tower at the eastern end of the site, with its street wall along Eighth Avenue. This would be the signature building, setting the design for the entire project. It would be the biggest office tower built in New York in decades, and Childs envisioned a monumental design in keeping with the great skyscrapers of the 1920s and 1930s.

For the residential component of the project, I went back to Frank Williams, our architect on the Columbia and several other projects. Frank designed a smaller tower thematically linked to Childs's office tower, along with a cluster of six- and seven-story townhouses scaled to the height of the existing structures along Ninth Avenue.

Paul Goldberger, architecture critic for the *New York Times*, was generous with his praise for our proposed design. He cited in particular the base of the office tower—"a handsome classical composition, its form enhanced by the soft curve of an elliptical shape that . . . reflects an elliptical public arcade inside the building." But he reserved his strongest accolades for the way the architects, in their overall plan, had forged a link between the office tower at one end of the site and the residential buildings at the other. "This design, like the best large-scale projects, aspires to being a connector, not a divider," Goldberger wrote, adding that it stood "at least a chance of being one of the few big projects that heals wounds in this cityscape instead of deepening them."

But we had work to do before that could happen. There was no question that this complex was going to change the neighborhood dramatically. The housing stock in Clinton was in terrible shape. Whatever tenements and brownstones on the blocks around our site hadn't been boarded up or taken over as flophouses were occupied largely by rent-controlled tenants, mostly the elderly and the working poor. The local residents had a vested interest in what happened in their neighborhood, and they were very vocal with their objections to our plans: the project was too big; development would force out existing residents and drive up prices in the area; the design was ugly. And I, as the developer, was the Bad Guy.

Negative opinions come with the territory: developers automatically get a bad rap because what we do inevitably means change. But I never liked being thought of as a bad guy. I tried always to be fair in my dealings, whether with an equity partner or a tenant facing relocation. I gained a reputation for being straightforward with local residents and listening to their concerns.

When I bought the Madison Square Garden site, I knew we would have to rehabilitate the side streets around it. We reached out to the community through Edith Fisher. She was a good listener and a good negotiator, practiced at dealing with local groups. She had established her worth on the Upper West Side and more recently in Union Square.

Here, the main issue for the residents was how much low-cost and middle-income housing we planned to give the community. Initially they asked for 20 percent of our residential buildings, but I persuaded them to accept renovated housing nearby instead. When we bought the site, six abandoned walk-ups across the street were part of the deal. I planned to renovate them for low-income neighborhood residents. I also planned to refurbish a number of small buildings that were currently occupied, both to benefit the residents and spruce up the neighborhood. Since upgrading the buildings would involve installing new plumbing and wiring, new bathrooms and kitchens, and new doors and windows, we would house the residents elsewhere while the work was going on. Rents on the apartments, which were well below market rate, would remain the same.

Faced with changes in their neighborhood, residents often are unclear about what's involved and unskilled at arguing for their rights, so much of Edith's work in Hell's Kitchen was educational. Eventually, most of the local residents accepted our plans, but there were a few who refused to budge even temporarily or tried

Rendering of Worldwide Plaza in a sales brochure

to squeeze us for big payouts. We had a legal obligation to ensure the well-being of the community. As long as we made a good-faith effort to provide appropriate relocation or compensation, we were in compliance with city regulations, even if the tenant refused our offer. These were not small concerns. Community groups have a voice before the official boards that are charged with green-lighting projects like ours, so we had a practical as well as a legal obligation to pay close attention to their needs.

Chief among the many ordinances and approvals on which a development rests are zoning regulations. Dizzyingly complex, they can be made more so by the variances a particular project requires. Our site was immediately west of the Midtown zone that allowed buildings of considerable height and volume as of right. We lacked those permissions, and to compound the problem, our site fell into three different zoning areas, each with its own specifications. When neighborhood opponents of our plans began invoking the discrepancies in the regulations to support their cause, I asked David Childs to sketch a plan for the site giving the maximum FAR—floor area ratio, or allowable height and volume in relation to footprint—if we adjusted for the restrictions of each zoning area. The sketch showed such a crazy quilt of building sizes and shapes that the community quickly reverted to considering our actual plans.

That did not, however, resolve other zoning constraints we faced. I began to meet regularly with Herb Sturz and other members of the City Planning Commission to find a way to build the size we needed to make the project profitable, while at the same time protecting the community. It helped our cause that my past projects, particularly Zeckendorf Towers, had improved their neighborhoods in tangible ways while being aesthetically sensitive to their surroundings. Eventually, with the CPC, I found a way to combine the various zoning requirements into one set of regulations that would cover both the office tower on Eighth Avenue and the residential buildings around Ninth Avenue.

We wanted to increase the FAR from the 10 allowed as of right to 12, so we could add eight floors to the office tower and gain an additional 320,000 square feet to lease. At $20 a square foot, that would increase our rental income by $6.4 million a year—even more as rents rose. Measured against the interest we were paying on our loans, that wasn't gold at the end of the rainbow, but our earnings would be more than adequate. The problem was how to justify the increase in FAR to the CPC. The planning commission had leeway to grant additional FAR to a developer whose project contained improvements that would benefit the city in general and the neighborhood in particular. We had already planned to include a one-acre landscaped public plaza in the middle of our site: that earned us a bonus FAR of 1. We also offered to rebuild the subway station under the office tower: that would get us another FAR. We would have done the subway renovations in any case: we needed a station worthy of a Class A office building with Class A tenants. We were looking for a way to gain one more FAR, but the City Planning Commission encouraged us to be content with 12.

The bonus FAR came with a catch. The city could prevent us from allowing tenants to occupy a certain number of floors until the public plaza and subway station were done. Terry Soderberg, who was project manager, kept this proviso in mind as he stepped up efforts to lease out the office space before the building went up.

Then we caught another lucky break. A broker called to ask if we could accommodate the law firm Cravath, Swaine & Moore. If we thought we'd struck gold in signing up Ogilvy & Mather, this was platinum: Cravath, Swaine & Moore was the quintessential old-line, white-shoe law firm, established in 1819. Their offices were downtown, in the heart of the Financial District. If they came to us, it would open up Midtown West not only to mavericks like Ogilvy & Mather but also to the ultra-conservative legal and financial community. Cravath wanted 350,000 square feet—fourteen or fifteen floors. That would cement Eighth Avenue as a prime destination for office space. Hardly daring to believe our good fortune, Terry and I crossed our fingers and began discussions with the law firm.

Cravath's current lease was due for renewal at a steep increase, and they needed more space. I arranged to take David Schwartz, the partner assigned to exploring the move, on a tour of the neighborhood. If the surroundings were going to scare him off, better to find out right away. Happily, he was undaunted by the decay and local landmarks like the Adonis Theater, a gay-porn movie house I assured him would be gone. (It was an assurance I wasn't able to make good on until 1994: the Adonis owner, a little Jewish grandmother named Chelly Wilson, was a tough negotiator.)

I continued to meet with Schwartz for more than a year, outlining what we could do for his firm. They wouldn't find rents as low as ours in a new building with the latest technology, I pointed out, and their space would, of course, be built to their specifications. Oh, and the 360-degree views. Zoning regulations that limited building around Worldwide Plaza meant that nothing would block those views for decades to come. Still, Schwartz had to sell the holdouts at Cravath on the benefits of trading the Financial District for Hell's Kitchen.

Mayor Ed Koch reviews a model of Worldwide Plaza with, from left, Bill Zeckendorf, Victor Elmaleh, and Frank Stanton

In the interim, we gave our project a name: Worldwide Plaza. We considered other names, but then my partners Victor Elmaleh and Frank Stanton told me, "You have Zeckendorf Towers and Zeckendorf Boulevard"—a street in Garden City, Long Island, named for my father. "Now we want our name on a building!" We settled on Worldwide Plaza, designating the office tower One Worldwide Plaza.

The city authorities approved our plans, and with SOM we selected HRH Construction, a subsidiary of Starrett, to manage construction. HRH in turn contracted with the dozens of trades responsible for every aspect of the building, from excavation to elevators to masonry to plumbing. We set the construction schedule and budget.

Two years after we bid on the site, the first shovel went into the ground. The groundbreaking ceremony on November 12, 1986, included representatives of the city, the community, our bankers, and the tenants, along with our architects and construction managers. Rituals like groundbreakings are a bit bogus: in this case, in order to stick to our construction schedule, we had begun construction days before the ceremony. I'm not much for long speeches, but I was expected to say a few words. I had planned to say, "Let's all break ground before we break some bread," but I forgot, so I mumbled something, we turned over a few spadefuls of dirt, and then went to a tent for refreshments.

This was the moment I usually stepped back from a work site. Once construction began, I headed back to the office to work on other projects. My passion—and gift—was putting together deals. I knew New York real estate cold: what sites were available; which ones were in negotiation or contention; which ones were not being used to their potential. I knew who owned what, who might want—or need—to sell. I knew what sites or parts of sites might fit together and how the zoning and abatements might work for or against me. I knew the minimum FAR on a project that would deliver a return and what price per square foot I could set. I knew where and how I could get financing for an assemblage—which banks and partners to approach—and how much money I could raise. And just as important as all that, I knew how to operate under the radar until I was ready to make my intentions known.

Moving on from a project under construction didn't mean I abandoned it altogether. I stayed in the loop at Worldwide, but I trusted Terry Soderberg and our site manager, Jack Schuster, to take care of day-to-day matters.

Meanwhile, my discussions with Cravath continued. They wanted an even lower rent than the already low figure we'd set for the building. I got the impression they thought *we* should be paying *them* to move into Worldwide. Given the prestige and increased marketability their presence would offer, they were probably right—up to a point. I held fast on the rent but offered to increase the work letter for the build-out of their floors. Still, we couldn't reach an agreement.

Then Viacom, the communications giant, came to Terry expressing interest in the floors Cravath was discussing. After much back and forth, Viacom was ready to move ahead. They negotiated a lease and a work letter. And then on October 19, 1987—"Black Monday"—the Dow Jones fell more than five hundred points. I figured Viacom would back out, but they struck a handshake deal, and I called Cravath to tell them that the space they'd been considering was gone.

Six weeks later, however, the stock market collapse caught up with Viacom, and they were forced to back out. Over the preceding year, we had signed up other sizable tenants besides Ogilvy & Mather—N. W. Ayer, another ad agency; Polygram, a recording company; and the New York office of Microsoft. But without Cravath or Viacom, the heart of the office tower, an immense amount of space, was empty. Construction was well under way, and once the building was complete, we wouldn't be able to afford empty space for even a month.

By that time, the office market was softening. So I went back to Cravath and gave them the lower rent they wanted, as well as a work letter for almost the same amount per square foot we were paying to construct the building. That left us with a 20 percent loss on Cravath's offices but at least the office tower was fully leased.

We should have been relieved, but now we had construction problems to contend with. Most office buildings going up in the 1980s had a metal skin, but David Childs's design called for brick. Which brick would be the biggest decision we made related to the building's design; the color of the brick alone was a point of contention that took months to resolve. Normally we would have gone with whatever color the architect recommended, but Victor Elmaleh, an architect by training though not in practice, had such strong feelings about the color that we let him duke it out with Childs. Victor wanted pink brick; David favored almond. Finally, they settled on three colors, for different parts of the building. We prepared to submit an order for 1.2 million bricks. It would be the largest brick job in the city's history.

Then the bids came in, well above what we'd estimated when we drew up the plans. It fell to me to negotiate the price. Masonry is the most expensive form of construction, so my strategy was to pretend we were considering a cheaper alternative. I reasoned that brick makers faced with no order at all would drop the price. Unfortunately, demand for brick in New York was high at that point, so we didn't get the price break we wanted. We ended up $1 million over budget on the bricks alone.

And that wasn't the end of the masonry problems. The bricks arrived late, which left the masons sitting on their trowels. Then there were problems in laying the bricks. In masonry construction, an air space is left between the bricks and the inner concrete wall of the building to prevent moisture from leaking into

Eighth Avenue facade of the Worldwide Plaza office tower

the interior. Any condensation that accumulates drains out through small openings in the brick called weep holes. However, the bricks delivered to our site had no weep holes. So a supervisor was following along behind the bricklayers, painting fake weep holes on the bricks. Fortunately, we discovered the ruse before bricks started popping off the building facade with disastrous consequences. But resolving the situation meant drilling weep holes in all the bricks, a time-consuming task. All the while, interest on our construction loan was mounting to the tune of $100,000 a day.

The stonework, too, was a circus of delays. Childs had designed an impressive oval base for the building with four separate lobbies, one for each of the main tenants. Linking the lobbies was a curvilinear arcade faced in granite with floors of polished marble. The granite was late in arriving, and the marble, quarried in Brazil and finished in Italy, was even later. We had to send a team over to Italy with the stone contractors to sort out the problem. Then the installation was nearly derailed by shoddy workmanship, causing further delays. Unfortunately, we had given the stonework contract to the lowest bidder, a company that turned out to be mob-owned—a fact brought home when the owner and other members of his "family" were sent to prison for price rigging.

There was another issue with the base, this one a flaw in the design. Childs's handsome two-story arcade with its soaring, thirty-five-foot ceilings served brilliantly as a means of connecting the four entryways, but the elliptical shape killed retail. It was almost impossible to lease the narrow, awkwardly configured spaces on the ground floor and mezzanine. Chase Bank took a small corner at $100 a square foot for an ATM, but we couldn't fill the rest. That cost us between $1 million and $2 million annually in lost revenue.

There were even more delays in constructing Worldwide Plaza's crowning feature, an octagonal copper cupola topped with a pyramid of clear glass—we took to calling it "the diamond"—that was lighted from within at night. Meanwhile, the subway station, part of a fragile transportation system caught in a web of city regulations, almost defied renovation. We had to carve out a new entrance and relocate major utility lines, but we eventually got it done, and the result was a vast improvement.

At the residential end of the site, construction proceeded without incident. Not so for condominium sales, which were not as strong as we'd hoped. In a sluggish market, the Ninth

Double-height arcade at the base of the office tower

Avenue location proved challenging. Between the tower and the townhouses we had 652 condos to fill, so we started a rental program to boost occupancy until sales picked up.

We were scheduled to finish Worldwide Plaza in November 1988. Ogilvy & Mather planned to move into their offices in December. But as delays mounted, it was obvious we weren't going to make the deadline. Terry Soderberg stepped in and negotiated us out of paying a late penalty. But it was May 1989 before Ogilvy could move in, and we lost $300,000 in rent in the meantime. And we still hadn't ironed out all the kinks in the building. Ogilvy was pleased with their space, but that didn't prevent them from complaining about things outside the building, like the plaza landscaping, which wasn't finished, and a sidewalk that hadn't been replaced. As it happened, both of these were casualties of the equipment hoist Ogilvy had installed for their build-out.

In the development business, you go from crisis to crisis, but Worldwide Plaza was six months late and $25 million over budget. Still, problems aside, the complex was a resounding success. We opened in 1989 with the office tower fully leased to Class A tenants, thereby legitimizing Eighth Avenue as a blue-chip corporate address. *Times* critic Paul Goldberger called the design "sumptuous" and compared what Worldwide Plaza had done for Eighth Avenue to what the Time & Life Building had done for Sixth Avenue decades earlier. On a broader scale, Worldwide Plaza redrew the cityscape: day or night, its distinctive copper crown is a landmark visible for miles around.

My biggest disappointment is that we finished Worldwide Plaza just as the real estate market was tanking. There was no way to avoid being caught in the backwash. A few tenants left, and when N. W. Ayer, with a lease worth $1 million a year, lost its biggest client, the agency filed for bankruptcy and stopped paying rent.

We eventually leased out the vacated floors, but because of the weak market, rents were below the original leases. We knew we needed to refinance or bring in another partner. Deutsche

"The diamond," the cupola atop the Worldwide Plaza office tower

Bank had given us a permanent mortgage of $550 million. We tried to refinance with them, but by then Deutsche Bank had decided to get out of real estate and turned us down. We brought in the Blackstone Group, one of the world's largest merchant banks, as a new general partner in the hope of structuring a plan amenable to all the parties, which included our developer partnership—Zeckendorf Company, World Wide Holdings, Arthur Cohen, and KG Land—and tenants with an ownership stake in the building. In the end, we couldn't work out an agreement, so Worldwide Plaza went to Blackstone.

What happened at Worldwide is a prime example of the risks inherent in real estate development. You might assemble

Night view of Worldwide Plaza

a site and build in one market, then find yourself dealing with tenant bankruptcies and unexpected vacancies in another, less favorable one. A complicated project can easily take ten or more years to come to fruition, exposing the developer to uncontrollable changes in market conditions.

Throughout the downturn, however, I remained convinced that a rebounding economy would restore Worldwide to profitability. I was right, though by that time I no longer had any stake in the complex. Worldwide Plaza was ahead of its time, but I never lost the conviction that Eighth Avenue was the future. In 1988, I predicted it would take five to ten years for it to take off. Add another decade, and that's pretty much what happened. By 2008, Eighth Avenue was just as I envisioned it, with corporate headquarters and Class A tenants filling office high-rises from the Time Warner Center on Columbus Circle and the Hearst Tower at West 57th Street all the way down to the *New York Times* headquarters at West 41st Street.

A Capital First

The Ronald Reagan Building and International Trade Center

Who would have guessed? The reception center in the Reagan Building—our project team used to call it "the wart" because it sticks out like a little bump on the eastern facade—is now one of Washington's most desirable venues for wedding receptions. It is also one of the most expensive.

TERRY SODERBERG, former senior VP and managing director, Zeckendorf Company

If a four-acre parking lot in Midtown Manhattan offered a prime opportunity to build a major project, how about an eleven-acre parking lot a block from the White House? In the spring of 1988, while we were pushing to finish Worldwide Plaza, I got a call from Bob Mendelsohn, a Washington, D.C., developer who was a member of the Federal City Council, an influential civic group. Would I be interested in becoming the lead developer on a significant project in the capital? The Pennsylvania Avenue Development Corporation was calling for proposals to design and construct a multiuse building on Pennsylvania Avenue, on the last open parcel in the jigsaw puzzle of government buildings known as the Federal Triangle. Mendelsohn's developer had pulled out, and he needed a big name to take his place.

The Federal Triangle project, which eventually became the Ronald Reagan Building and International Trade Center, was a massive, multiyear undertaking. The program called for a 3.1-million-square-foot structure with 2 million square feet of offices, a trade center, theaters, space for cultural exhibits, and underground parking for more than 2,000 cars. It would be second in size only to the Pentagon, Washington's largest federal office building, and it would be the first building in the capital to house both public agencies and private enterprises under one roof. As soon as I realized the scope of the project, I asked a good friend, Larry Silverstein, to be my co-developer. Bob Mendelsohn had already brought in Fred Nicholas, a shopping center and office complex developer from Los Angeles.

Efforts to finish building out the Federal Triangle had been decades in the making. In the 1920s, work began on a master plan to upgrade Pennsylvania Avenue between the Capitol and the White House. Building stopped during the Depression for lack of funds. In the 1960s, President John F. Kennedy envisioned completing construction, but it was not until the 1980s that the right people came together to get the project under way again.

Kenneth Sparks, executive vice president of the Federal City Council, had long been talking up the idea of establishing an international trade center. Then in 1986, Terence Golden, the new head of the General Services Administration, which oversees federal buildings, picked up on the idea of a giant office complex as a cost-saving measure—a way to consolidate hundreds of federal offices spread all over the city—and suggested the Federal Triangle site. Senator Daniel P. Moynihan, chair of the subcommittee overseeing public building, got behind the project. As secretary of labor, he had worked with President Kennedy on redeveloping Pennsylvania Avenue.

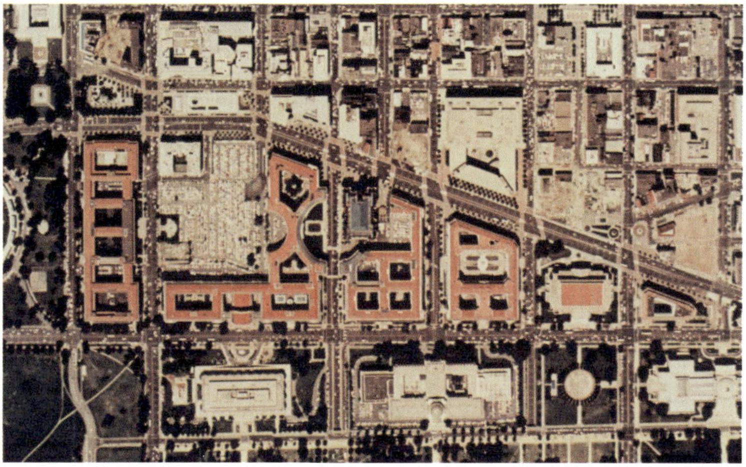

Aerial view of the Federal Triangle before construction of the Ronald Reagan Building

Moynihan had sponsored legislation that would allow the federal government to build without spending public money up front. But the administration decided to fund the project after all. In 1987, Congress authorized construction of the complex, appropriated $362 million for the project, and put the PADC in charge of creating the International Cultural and Trade Center Commission. Initially, the PADC was assigned to manage the building and lease out 500,000 square feet for cultural events and exhibitions. Later politics took over—this was Washington, after all—and the GSA decided it wanted in, so management was shared by the PADC and the GSA.

The PADC was charged with selecting the development team. They put out a request for proposals—what's known as an RFP. Some thirty teams had formed to look at the RFP, and ten were thought to be submitting proposals. The exercise was not cheap: submission would end up costing between $750,000 and $1 million. In the end, only seven teams prepared proposals, among them Skidmore, Owings & Merrill, Kohn Pedersen Fox, and Michael Graves. The one that worried me the most was Kohn Pedersen Fox. My old friend and rival George Klein was the lead developer, and their construction firm, Bechtel, was not only one of the largest construction companies in the world but also had an in with the federal government: Bechtel's president was

James Freed, architect of the Ronald Reagan Building (top)

Terry Soderberg, Zeckendorf Company development manager for the Ronald Reagan Building

George Shultz, who had been secretary of State, Labor, and the Treasury and, before that, director of the Office of Management and Budget.

The most important criterion for the project was design. The architect for our group, designated the Delta Group, was James Ingo Freed. A partner at Pei Cobb Freed, he was one of the most talented architects I've ever known. Jim had recently designed the United States Holocaust Memorial Museum in the capital. Quite an undertaking for a Jewish architect who had escaped Nazi Germany when he was nine. Associates from the Washington office of Ellerbe Becket, an architectural and engineering firm, were responsible for the working drawings. Perini was the general contractor.

I had my first meeting with our team in Washington about two months before the final presentation. It was a huge group, with architects, civil engineers, structural engineers, soil engineers, and landscape architects. Each technical group was also required to bring in a minority-led firm as its associate. After the selection process was completed and we had signed the development agreement, the government hired Tishman to liaise with our development team as the construction consultant. This led to some friction later, when construction problems on the Rihga Royal Hotel surfaced and Kumagai Gumi, our partner on the hotel, initiated a legal action against Tishman. At that point Tishman started dragging their heels on government approvals; when Kumagai dropped the suit, the delays stopped.

Unlike most of my projects, the Reagan Building was a "fee development" project. That meant we would be paid a fee as lead developer and all related fees, including salaries, D.C. office rent, and health insurance, would be capped. I asked Terry Soderberg to be our on-site development manager. He commuted weekly for the first two years, then moved to Washington and put together a team, running the project from an office across Pennsylvania Avenue from the construction site.

In July 1988, a month after submitting our entry, we received notice that the PADC was ready to consider the proposals. Presentations were scheduled for early September. Our design and development team spent two days holed up in a conference room at the offices of Ellerbe Becket, feverishly preparing. On day two, we worked until 3:30 AM, stopping just six hours before we were scheduled to present.

All the partners were there for the rehearsal, along with twenty-five or so people from the technical teams. Jim Freed's drawings were set up on boards around the conference room. They were magnificent. Jim suffered from Parkinson's disease and had great difficulty moving around. During the rehearsal, he had such pronounced tremors that he couldn't hold a pointer still enough for any of us to follow it. Everyone was trying to figure out an alternative—maybe someone else could point to details on the drawings while Jim described them, it was suggested. But I said no, we should let Jim go ahead with the presentation. If he waved the pointer all over the place, it would force the audience to pay closer attention.

Finally, it was presentation day, and our turn had come. After the usual introductions, the meeting was turned over to Jim. Everyone held their breath. But forget Jim's affliction. Suddenly he was like a kangaroo, jumping from one drawing to the next while he excitedly explained the principles of his design. Arms flying, he demonstrated how he had fulfilled the requirement to integrate the exterior of the building with the Federalist architecture along Pennsylvania Avenue while creating a totally modern office building behind the traditional facade.

Jim Freed had initially seemed an unlikely choice for the project: he was a renowned modernist whose design for the Reagan Building was, by his own description, the "least Beaux-Arts" of those submitted, "a contemporary reading of the neoclassical style." What won over the judges, however, were elements like the magnificent vaulted atrium connecting the 14th Street and Woodrow Wilson Plaza entrances and the domed rotunda marking the formal entrance to the International Trade Center.

Our presentation to the PADC directors took about two hours. A month later, we were notified that the board was meeting to

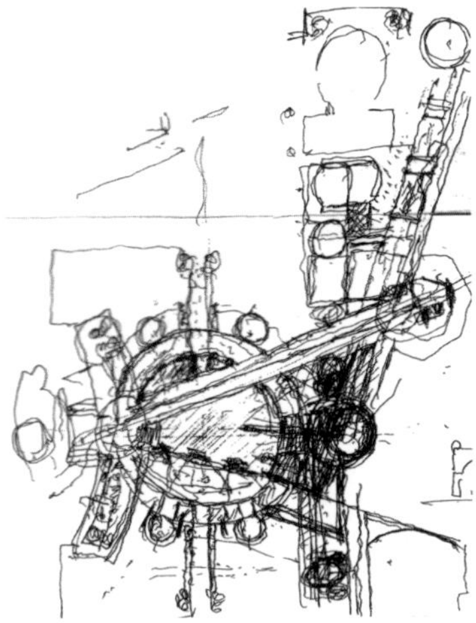

Sketch of the floor plan for the Ronald Reagan Building

select a plan; each team was invited to send two representatives to observe the voting. Terry Soderberg and Bob Mendelsohn were our group's. On the appointed day, the directors went into closed session for three hours, then opened the meeting to the observers for the vote. Terry still recalls what happened:

> All morning we were sequestered in separate offices. Finally we were called into the conference room. We were standing in the back; there were no chairs for us. There were fifteen directors in all, but one was absent and another abstained because of a potential conflict of interest. So there were going to be thirteen votes. The chair described a complicated voting procedure involving several ballots. Then they started going around the table. I was standing in the back counting the number of votes for Delta: one, two . . . Then I heard the chairman say, "On the first ballot we have a winner. The results are X for this team, Y for that team, and seven for the winner, Delta." I turned to Bob and said, "Oh, shit. Now we have to build the thing!"
>
> I called our office in New York and found out that Bill was in a meeting at Manufacturers Hanover. "Get him!" I told Marge, our office manager. She transferred the call to Manny Hanny, and I could hear Bill in the background saying gruffly, "What's Terry calling for?" When he got on the phone, I told him, "Bill, we won!" "Won what?" was all he said. "The competition," I reminded him. "I'll be back tomorrow."

Winning the competition was just the beginning. This was by far the biggest project we had ever taken on. The size and scope would have challenged any team of builders, but dealing with the federal government ratcheted everything up a notch. One of the first things we needed was a good attorney to negotiate for us. We poached Joe Fries from one of the other teams. Fries was a partner in Arent Fox, a Washington firm that specialized in complicated real estate deals. Just how complicated was hammering out our agreement with the government? Terry Soderberg recalls precisely: it took 112 days, 16 hours, and 22 minutes.

We finally started construction in January 1991. The excavation and underground garage alone took two years. We first had to build a concrete slurry wall three feet thick and one hundred feet deep around the entire eleven acres, creating a kind of bathtub that would prevent water from pouring into the construction site and what would eventually be the garage. Each panel of the concrete slurry wall had to be put in place in a continuous pour, then left to dry before the next panel was poured. Each pour went on for hours, and just about every cement truck in the District and its environs had to be pressed into service—twenty-two trucks per panel.

Once construction was under way, I took the shuttle down to Washington every month or so to check on progress. But Terry was the one on the firing line, working not only with the architects, engineers, construction supervisors, and subcontractors but also with the PADC, the GSA, and members of the International Trade Center—all political appointees—as well as future tenants like the Environmental Protection Agency, the U.S. Agency for International Development, U.S. Customs, and the Justice

Aerial view of the Ronald Reagan Building, Washington, D.C.

View of the Ronald Reagan Building from across Pennsylvania Avenue

Department. It was a monumental job that he handled with great skill.

Construction was supposed to take about four years. Instead it dragged on far longer. The building wasn't dedicated until 1998, and Terry didn't sign the last construction document until June 2003. All told, the project took fifteen years from the day we entered the competition to the final signoff by our partnership and the GSA. In our initial proposal, we budgeted the cost at $756 million, including financing. When the federal government decided to self-finance, we told them we would bring it in at $730 million; the final figure was $736 million. Inflation accounted for some of the additional cost, but much of the overrun in time and money was the result of repeated changes in the plans. Even after we'd begun construction, the whole program shifted. The cultural component was scaled back and the office space enlarged.

Originally, there was to be a state-of-the-art 2,300-seat theater in the building, but the Kennedy Center for the Performing

Atrium of the Ronald Reagan Building

Arts, located nearby, objected to any competition. They forced a dramatic downscaling of the theater: maximum capacity is now 625. Redrawing the plans for that change alone cost $500,000. And that wasn't the end of the revisions. The government tenants kept switching, and once the building was above ground and everyone could see how magnificent it was going to be, other federal agencies and departments clamored to get in. The EPA, USAID, and Customs remained, but by the time we opened, one of the very first tenants, Justice, had backed out, while the Woodrow Wilson International Center for Scholars was in.

For Freed, the challenge was to accommodate governmental and private tenants with vastly different needs. USAID, the largest of the federal tenants, had already moved in when they asked us to redesign their offices without windows, for security reasons. We didn't—it would have looked terrible and added even more time and money to the construction budget. Instead we installed double-paned windows with a shatterproof coating. Freed weathered all the changes, earning everyone's respect for the way he handled refinements of his plans.

Changes in the plans weren't the only problem we faced. The sheer size of the project made it hard to get firm bids from subcontractors, and there were few companies large enough to bid in the first place.

In 1995, the building officially became the Ronald Reagan Building and International Trade Center: Congress had decided to name the building after former President Reagan since he was in office when the project was approved. The dedication ceremony, on May 5, 1998, was an impressive affair, in keeping with the importance of the building. Nancy Reagan was a speaker at the dedication, along with President Bill Clinton and Senator Moynihan, who had been so influential in making the complex a reality. Others on the dais included former senator Bob Dole and Ken Sparks of the Federal City Council, along with a handful of senators and representatives of several federal agencies. Jim Freed and I represented our team. The program for the ceremony acknowledged the "visionaries who foresaw the importance of completing the Federal Triangle, the last undeveloped land parcel on the nation's 'Main Street' (Pennsylvania Avenue)" and the "legislators who enabled that vision to become a reality" and cited the "efforts of business leaders in Washington who realized the importance of establishing a world trade center in the nation's capital."

Afterward, we got a lot of flack from our partners about the building dedication plaque affixed to the limestone wall near the 14th Street entrance. Alongside the names of various government officials is a listing that reads, "Federal Triangle Corporation:

Nancy Reagan speaking at the dedication of the Ronald Reagan Building, 1998

William Zeckendorf Jr., president; Terry Soderberg, development manager." No Fred Nicholas. No Larry Silverstein. No Bob Mendelsohn. "This is going to be a problem," Terry told me, and he was right. At the dedication, Fred took a picture of the plaque. He sent it to me later, very upset. Terry wrote to Fred and Larry: "I gave all your names to GSA. It was their decision what went on the plaque. It's been up for two years." I always wondered if the omission had anything to do with the fact that during the entire construction period, neither Larry nor Fred nor Bob visited the site more than five or six times.

Despite the fuss over the plaque, it's safe to say that for our entire team, developing the Ronald Reagan Building was a once-in-a-lifetime experience. Awarded a 1998 GSA Design Award, the building is an outstanding finish to the Federal Triangle and a noteworthy landmark for Washington, D.C.

Turnaround in Queens

Citylights

New York is clearly a stronger, better, more vibrant city because of Bill. He didn't primarily build for poor people but he wasn't building for the rich. He was building for working-class people. And the idea of having this kind of development for people to live and work in the city was important to him.

HERB STURZ, former chair, New York City Planning Commission, and partner in Citylights

There's a classic photo of my father in an overcoat and hat, standing in a field of rough grass with the United Nations Secretariat in the distance behind him. That field is almost the exact spot in Queens where a few decades later I built one of my last big projects, Citylights. A forty-two-story apartment tower, Citylights was the first building in Queens West, a seventy-four-acre mixed-use waterfront development in the Hunters Point section of Long Island City. It was an ambitious project aimed at transforming an industrial wasteland into a desirable residential, office, and recreational area.

Citylights pioneered in more ways than one. A stunning building by the renowned architect Cesar Pelli, it set the bar high not only for Queens West but for affordable housing in general, offering world-class design, upscale amenities, and spectacular views at prices within reach of middle-income buyers. The financing, too, was a first: an ingenious and daring public-private arrangement that paved the way for a new form of construction loan.

Citylights was also the first time I partnered with Herb Sturz, a pioneer in his own right. As chairman of the City Planning Commission from 1979 to 1986, Herb had been helpful to me on several projects. In the process, he became a good friend. Herb is widely respected for his innovative social service work. As I got to know him, I could see why. The essence of Herb is summed up in two words: character and determination.

I met Herb through a mutual friend, Howard Stein. An innovator in mutual funds, Howard was president of the Dreyfus Corporation at the time. He invited Herb and me to lunch at his townhouse in the East 70s. After Herb left the CPC, Howard suggested that the three of us partner on a development project. The idea intrigued me, and I agreed to look for something suitable.

As Herb remembers it, the plan really came together one weekend when he and I and our wives were staying with the Steins at their house in Southampton, Long Island. By then I had assembled some land along the East River in Queens and was in talks with the New York State Urban Development Corporation about being lead developer on a large-scale project that the UDC—along with the Port Authority of New York and New Jersey and New York City's Public Development Corporation—was planning for Hunters Point.

The project had been brewing in government offices since 1983, and in 1986 the Gruzen Partnership, working with the architects Beyer Blinder Belle, had released a master plan combining low-rise housing with public space built on decks over

William Zeckendorf Sr. in Queens, with the United Nations in the background

the East River. But when the real estate market collapsed in the late 1980s, the project was shelved. In 1991, Mario Cuomo, then governor of New York, set up the Queens West Development Corporation to oversee the project. At that point the Zeckendorf Company controlled approximately one-quarter of the land in the development area.

The site was spectacular, with a panoramic view of the Manhattan skyline, and there was an excellent subway connection nearby. But the property itself was a dump. The most visible structure was the huge neon Pepsi-Cola sign on top of the Pepsi bottling plant, a last vestige of this once thriving industrial area. (There's an oft-repeated tale that Joan Crawford, the widow of Pepsi CEO Alfred Steele, had ordered that the Pepsi sign be erected in full view of River House, a posh co-op across the East River in Manhattan. Allegedly this was in retaliation for being blackballed by the co-op board, whose president at the time, Robert Woodruff, had been CEO of Coca-Cola. A great story, but an unlikely one: the Pepsi sign went up in 1938, long before Crawford married Steele.)

Herb Sturz had promoted development of Hunters Point while he was working for the city, never dreaming that one day he would be directly involved. I proposed to Herb and Howard that our first joint venture be a residential tower in Queens West—stage one of the master plan.

Once again, I was trailblazing. By then it was clear that this was what I enjoyed most and did best. For that, Howard and Herb were ideal partners.

We put Herb in charge. He had no development experience, but his years at the CPC had taught him a lot about zoning, design, and community pressure and had honed his commitment to socially responsible urban planning. His persistence and optimism would be invaluable in overcoming obstacles in such a complex project.

Howard and Herb formed Trotwood Corporation, a subsidiary of Dreyfus named after Herb's standard poodle. Then, with my longtime partners World Wide Holdings and Arthur Cohen, I joined with Trotwood to form Manhattan Overlook Associates. Rounding out our development group were Martin Raynes, head of a management company, and investment banker James Wolfensohn, who connected us with two Japanese construction companies, Tekken and Tobishima. Howard Stein came up with the name Citylights: very appropriate for a building that had sweeping views of the lights of Manhattan at night and would itself be a beacon on the Queens skyline.

Initially, I brought in Frank Williams as our architect: he had done such good work for me on other projects. But given the location, we knew there were challenges ahead. Having a marquee architect would help us secure financing and government approvals, as well as market the apartments. Victor Elmaleh suggested Cesar Pelli. Herb was instrumental in persuading Pelli to accept the commission.

Our market would be largely middle-income. The challenge was to create a quality building for people of modest means in an untried location where the primary asset was the view. Luckily, Pelli was sufficiently intrigued by the challenge to come on board. I still wanted to involve Frank, but we couldn't have two architects, and we needed Pelli's vision and clout. I didn't have the heart to tell Frank, though. Herb had to do it.

Pelli collaborated on the design with Peter Claman of Schuman Lichtenstein Claman Efron. Claman knew the regu-

Cesar Pelli, architect of Citylights (top)

Herb Sturz, development partner

Pepsi-Cola sign, Long Island City

lations associated with government loans—they had an arcane way of measuring space, for one thing—which would be a major consideration in the financing. Plus, he was a master of apartment layouts, and designing from the inside out had become a Zeckendorf trademark. Pelli and his son Rafael designed a beautiful skin to wrap around Claman's floor plans. Pelli oriented the building so that the longer side was perpendicular to the shoreline. Parallel would have been the more conventional solution, but this innovative positioning meant that most of the rooms had river views.

The amenities included a garage, a health club, and tennis courts. Just as at Battery Park City, an esplanade runs along the river in front of the building. A short distance away is Gantry Plaza State Park, the first public space in the Queens West development. It was named for, and designed around, two gantries—giant black hoists once used to transfer railroad cars from barges to the Long Island Railroad yard.

Beyer Blinder Belle's master plan for Queens West had initially centered on low-rise buildings; the community was vigorously opposed to bringing Manhattan-style luxury development to Queens, fearing it would push out the middle class. Pelli, however, did a masterful job of convincing QWDC that high-rise towers like the one we were building would yield better urban

Citylights, Queens, with gantries in the foreground

design than the low- and midrise courtyard scheme originally envisioned. Jack Beyer, principal of BBB, quickly embraced Pelli's design and was instrumental in modifying the master plan to permit construction of Citylights. Since then, a revised master plan has unleashed a flood of new construction along Long Island City's waterfront, with buildings twice the size of ours.

Model of Citylights

The master plan required us to construct 40,000 square feet of retail. That was risky, given that ours was the first building in what was to be a twenty-building development; we knew retailers would be reluctant to lease space before more buildings went up. We convinced QWDC to let us build a public elementary school instead. Then we arranged for the Board of Education to lease 30,000 square feet; with their funding, we built a 300-student facility on the first two floors of Citylights. The school now serves as a major amenity for the community.

Because of the geology of the waterfront, we had to set the foundation on friction piles, using the surrounding soil rather than bedrock for support. We began constructing the foundations even before we took possession of a corner of the site occupied by Hobart, the food equipment company. Hobart agreed to move, so we found them a suitable building nearby and retrofitted it just in time to raze the old building and finish the Citylights foundation.

The main parcel of our assemblage was the former Long Island Railroad yard, where the air rights were controlled by New York City, or more specifically, QWDC. We structured a sale-and-leaseback deal with QWDC that allowed us to build a tower of the size we wanted and get the real estate tax abatement we needed to make the project work.

Frederick Harris, vice president of Trotwood, undertook the job of financing the project. No bank would risk making a loan for construction in that location. We briefly considered New York State tax-exempt bonds, but there were too many restrictions involved. Herb suggested we apply to the Federal Housing Administration. The FHA, which is part of the Department of Housing and Urban Development, doesn't lend money, but it insures mortgages against default, thereby reducing the risk for lenders. At that time, however, the FHA funded only rental development. Herb went to work.

He came up with a strategy that had never been tried before—it was the most creative financing I'd ever seen. The plan was that we would finance the project as a rental, with an

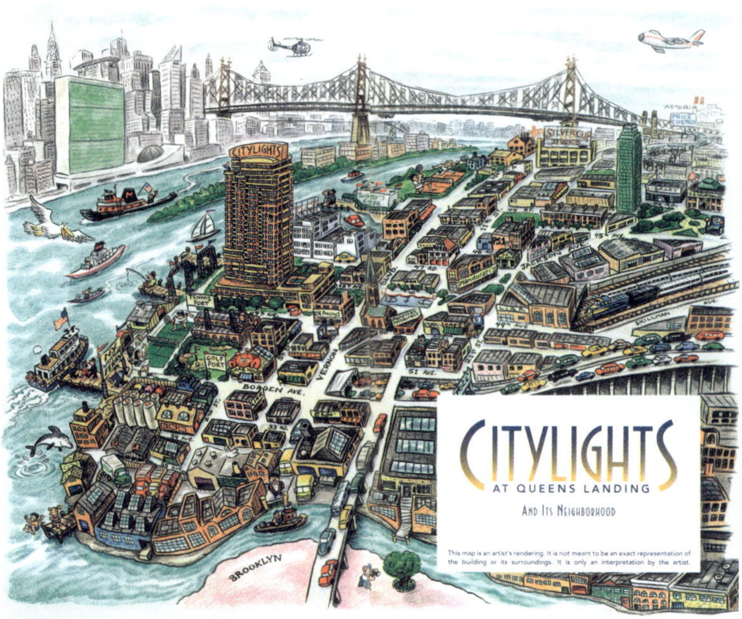

Drawing of Citylights and surrounding area from a sales brochure

FHA-guaranteed loan, then convert the building to a co-op and sell shares. Because of the underlying financing, the initial cash outlay for buyers would be quite low—as little as $8,000 for a studio on a low floor and up to $90,000 or so for a two-bedroom unit high in the tower.

Once Herb gets an idea, he never lets up. I don't know how many trips to Washington, D.C., he had to make to convince the FHA that this arrangement was legal—or how he and Fred managed to overcome HUD's disbelief that we could charge such low prices. But in the process of pushing this idea through Washington, Herb and Fred came up with a whole new method of financing construction based on a combination of government and private lending.

The FHA mortgage insurance allowed us to borrow $85.6 million for construction from the AFL-CIO Housing Investment Trust; upon completion of the project, the loan converted to a fixed-rate forty-year mortgage. If the cash outlay for an apartment was, say, $50,000, the buyer's share of the underlying mortgage might be $140,000, which could be paid down in installments as part of the regular monthly maintenance fee. Alternatively, the buyer could finance the mortgage payment through an outside lender.

These terms made apartment owning possible for a wide range of buyers, just as we had intended. The initial occupants of Citylights were a diverse lot, from first-time homeowners in studios to wealthy residents combining two or more units.

As successful at development as Herb Sturz proved to be, for-profit real estate was ultimately not for him. Citylights was his first and last project with us. Around the time we finished construction, Herb was tapped by George Soros's Open Society Foundations to arrange financing to build 300,000 homes for low-income families in South Africa. Herb has been with Open Society ever since as a board member and advisor, working on after-school programs, criminal justice, and other projects aimed at making this a better world.

As for Citylights, I'm pleased to note that in 1998, the year after it opened, the building won HUD's John J. Gunther Blue Ribbon Award for Best Practices in Housing and Community Development, the highest honor in the field.

The Hotel Maven

The company grew fast, and by the mid-1980s, what had been a lean organization with eight or nine people had mushroomed into a bustling enterprise with forty or fifty people on the payroll. Between 1985 and the end of the decade, we had more projects on the books than any other developer in New York. I was in the office by 7:00 every morning, and it wasn't unusual for me to stay until midnight.

Not only were we building a lot but we were also entering competitions. We lost one to replace the Coliseum on Columbus Circle, but in July 1985, we edged out seven other teams to win a major commission: developing South Ferry Plaza at the southern tip of Manhattan. This was a $400 million public-private joint venture. We were to rebuild the existing ferry terminal and put an office tower on top of it. Frank Williams designed the winning entry: sixty stories of pink granite, crowned with a glass dome. We poured a tremendous amount of effort—and $1 million—into the project. New York owned the land and stood to gain millions from the ninety-nine-year ground lease alone.

But the city dragged its heels and finally, in 1991, scrapped the plans altogether. We were disappointed, but we may have been saved from a greater disappointment: the economy had turned, and leasing office space would have been hard, even in a prime Lower Manhattan location.

There's a famous photo of my father in the back seat of his limousine, talking on the phone. I'm told he was the first private citizen in the United States to have a phone in his car, and true to form, he had not one but two. By the 1980s, I was following suit. A reporter for the *New York Times* who rode around with me for a story called my car phone "crucial" to my operation. He was right. I saw no point in sitting behind a desk in the office, crunching numbers. Like my father, I carried all the facts and figures in my head and could just as easily do deals from the back of my silver-blue limo.

Although mixed-use projects and condominiums were my focus in those years, I never put hotels entirely out of mind. My earliest successes had been hotel renovations, but this time around I was partnering with established hotel operators and building from the ground up. I still had no interest in being in the hospitality business: once a hotel was finished, I wanted to sell it and move on. Still, I had an eye for a good property, and if I thought the best use of it was for a hotel, then that's what I would build.

The three hotels I developed in the 1980s and early 1990s couldn't have been more different deals or designs.

Lighting Up Times Square

The Crowne Plaza Hotel

Bill just has a knack, a gift that cannot be quantified or codified, for spotting a neighborhood that's ripe for change, coupled with the resolve to put his money and reputation on the line and build the catalyst that will produce that change. None of the feasibility experts, focus groups, and other esoteric and mysterious studies can come close to the instincts of a truly talented entrepreneur.

ALAN LAPIDUS, *Everything by Design: My Life as an Architect*

During the 1980s, the New York City Planning Commission launched a campaign to shift high-rise development from the East Side to Midtown West. Around the same time, city and state officials created the 42nd Street Development Project to remake thirteen acres around Times Square. By then, West 42nd Street was no longer the legendary center of American theater but a string of peep shows, burlesque joints, and xxx-rated movie houses, populated by hookers, junkies, and homeless sleeping in the doorways. Even the beat cops hated patrolling the area.

Going up Broadway from Times Square, the landscape wasn't much better. Legitimate theaters were all but crowded out by the porn industry. To encourage new building that would upgrade the Times Square district, the city revised the zoning laws.

Working with real estate broker Bob Shapiro, I put together land on Broadway between West 48th and 49th Streets, a block from Worldwide Plaza, for a 770-room luxury hotel, the Crowne Plaza. When the hotel opened in 1989, we were widely applauded for cleaning up a particularly blighted part of the Times Square area. In his book *Everything by Design*, our architect, Alan Lapidus, described just how seedy the property was when we bought it: "This block had the densest collection of xxx-rated theaters and related enterprises in the city, including that paragon of porn, the Pussycat Theater."

Bob had first spotted the potential for an assemblage on that block in 1977, when a four-story building at the corner of Broadway and 48th Street came on the market. A year later he began discussions with Mickey Zaffarano, a former bodyguard for Mafia boss Joe Bonanno, who owned a string of porn shops and movie theaters north of the corner building. But in 1980, Zaffarano dropped dead in his office just as the feds were coming to arrest him, and Bob set aside the assemblage idea and went to work for Merrill Lynch. When Bob reopened his firm, City Center Real Estate, a few years later, the Zaffarano property was in play. Jason Carter, my partner on two of the Battery Park City condos, owned the Ritz Theater on West 48th Street, adjacent to the Zaffarano holdings, and approached Bob about putting together a development site.

Carter at the time had his eye on the lot west of the Ritz, where Mamma Leone's restaurant stood, but Bob persuaded him to look east instead. Bob brokered a sale of the Zaffarano property, with Jason agreeing to pay John Zaffarano, Mickey's son, $3 million to clear up any liens and another $500,000 to settle his debts. Then Jason brought me into the deal, along with my partners, World Wide Holdings and Arthur Cohen. Later, we brought in Elie Hirschfeld, my partner in Zeckendorf Towers; Zev Wolfson, one of my partners on the ill-fated South Ferry project; and KG Land.

The sale very nearly didn't happen, though. In our first meeting with John Zaffarano, Arthur Cohen tried to change the terms, and Zaffarano threatened to walk out. Arthur and Jason and I retreated to a conference room while Bob tried to calm down Zaffarano. It was Friday afternoon, and I was set to leave for our country house. Instead, I decided to stick it out. I had just struck a deal with the Holiday Corporation, owner of Holiday Inns and Embassy Suites, to build a hotel on the site, but Holiday was being aggressively courted by developer Bruce Eisner to build the hotel on *his* property nearby, so I wasn't about to let the Zaffarano deal get away.

Arthur Cohen relented, and we all agreed on the terms. But when the contract arrived for signing, problems emerged. Not only were there the liens on the Zaffarano property that we'd already agreed to pay but there was also a mortgage that was in default and about to be foreclosed. Zaffarano had thought he could deliver the property empty, except for a gay bathhouse. It ended up costing us close to $300,000 to buy the bathhouse lease. And then we had to advance Zaffarano the money to buy out leases on a porn bookstore and a couple of movie houses, in addition to paying his outstanding water and sewer taxes.

The Pussycat Theater near Times Square

Rendering of the Crowne Plaza Hotel

Bob had also brokered a deal for us to purchase another property on the block, the Mardi Gras, a topless bar and grill. In the meantime, the owner, Matthew Ianniello—better known as Matty the Horse—had been indicted for skimming profits and ripping off Con Edison, so the U.S. Attorney's office had taken over his property. We had to meet with Rudy Giuliani, then U.S. Attorney for the Southern District of New York, to assure him that our purchase offer was aboveboard.

In June 1985 we finally signed the contract of sale. We now owned 1601 Broadway, which included the Mardi Gras and a porn movie house; 1603–7 Broadway, home of the gay bathhouse, the bookstore, and the Pussycat Theater; and a gay movie theater at 207 West 48th Street. We then bought a four-story garage at 217 West 48th Street—a deal that went through without a hitch. The owner, Sol Goldman, was my partner on some other projects.

That still left us missing a critical piece of the assemblage: a building at 209 West 49th Street occupied by Magno Sound, the largest post-production film company in New York. We couldn't build without it, but Magno had nearly completed a major renovation, and the owner refused to sell. Luckily, Bob Shapiro not only is a shrewd negotiator but also has a great sense of humor. That's what finally persuaded Magno's owner, Ralph Friedman, to sell. Bob remembers:

> My conversations with Mr. Friedman were like a Pandora's box, because every time he presented a problem and we were able to solve it, backed up with data and analysis, he would come up with another problem. In order to change his attitude, I called up a balloon service and ordered the biggest bunch of helium balloons they carried and had them delivered to Mr. Friedman. Written across the balloons were the words "air rights"—if all else failed, I would try to do an air rights deal with Friedman and then back into a sales position. With the balloons I sent a note that said, "You don't write, you don't call, you don't visit." The day after the balloons were delivered, I did my normal routine of showing up at Magno and trying to see Mr. Friedman. When I got to the

office, everyone from the receptionist to Mr. Friedman's secretaries greeted me with a great deal of warmth and humor. Then Mr. Friedman came out, laughed at me, and said, "You are too much." He agreed to do something: he said he just needed time to "work out his thoughts."

Whenever I met with Mr. Friedman, his executive secretary would remark on how conservatively I was dressed, in my investment-banker gray. The atmosphere at Magno was very informal; most people wore polo shirts. To get into the swing of things, I began to show up in a satin *Miami Vice* jacket with a flamingo-pink lining that I had appropriated from my nephew Brandon Tartikoff, then president of NBC Entertainment.

Bob finally convinced Friedman that his present facilities weren't adequate for his growing company and worked out a plan to move Magno into larger quarters nearby. I offered Friedman $8 million for his building, but he wanted $14 million. I was ready to walk away from the deal, but Bob got us to agree on $10 million. We finally closed in May 1986—more than a year after Bob started working on Friedman.

There were two pieces of the assemblage we weren't able to buy outright: the four-story building on the West 48th Street corner and a restaurant on the 49th Street corner owned by the Riese Organization. We needed the properties to fill out the blockfront, so we signed a ninety-nine-year ground lease on each property and also bought air rights from Riese. For his efforts in putting together our complicated assemblage, Bob Shapiro deservedly won the Real Estate Board of New York's Most Ingenious Deal of the Year Award in 1986.

In all, we spent about $60 a square foot to purchase the land parcels and ground leases that made up the site—a good price considering the location. Most of the hotels around Times Square in those days were the kind that rented rooms by the hour, but I was confident there was an emerging market for upscale accommodations. Here was another chance to help transform a derelict corner of New York. A Marriott hotel

Alan Lapidus, architect of the Crowne Plaza Hotel

was already going up on Broadway when I struck the deal with the Holiday Corporation. Holiday decided to call our hotel the Crowne Plaza and make it the flagship of their newest chain.

We financed construction of the hotel with a $227 million loan from a consortium of banks organized by First Chicago Bank and Scotiabank. Arranging the financing was challenging because we owned only part of the site outright and the rest consisted of ground leases. But because of my reputation for successfully building complicated development projects, I was able to secure the necessary loan.

I signed Tishman as our construction firm and then, at John Tishman's suggestion, hired Alan Lapidus as our architect. Alan was an inspired choice. He had worked for years with his father, Morris Lapidus, the king of glitzy, over-the-top hotel design, famously showcased in Miami Beach stalwarts like the Eden Roc and the Fontainebleau.

Alan later told the *New York Times* that his design for the forty-six-story Crowne Plaza was inspired by the Wurlitzer jukebox, an Art Deco icon of the 1930s. The hotel was certainly more flamboyant than anything else I had built, but it was perfect for the campaign to restore Broadway as the "Great White Way." We were in the midst of designing the hotel when the city enacted new legislation intended to restore the energy and pizzazz of Times Square as a legendary entertainment capital. Ours was the first new construction subject to the "razzle-dazzle" regulations, which required all new buildings on Broadway and Seventh Avenue from West 42nd to 50th Street to plaster brightly lighted commercial signs all over their facades.

There was ample precedent for razzle-dazzle on our site: the Pussycat Theater sign was a marvel of flashing neon with letters six feet tall until we tore it down in 1986. Working with lighting consultants, Alan Lapidus and the rest of our team figured out how to install 20,000 square feet of neon and mixed-media signage with minimal impact on the functionality of the building. We were just north of the highly visible junction of Broadway and Seventh Avenue, which made it hard to attract advertis-

Broadway facade of the Crowne Plaza Hotel, New York

ing at first. So we had to build the signs on spec—a whopping $1 million investment. Fortunately, advertisers eventually caught on, and the signs became a lucrative source of income. Meanwhile, the technology we pioneered set the standard for illuminating facades on Broadway from then on.

Along with the banks of neon lighting, the Crowne Plaza design reflected Lapidus's sense of whimsy. For cost reasons, we

Lighted signs on the Crowne Plaza Hotel

toned down the most exuberant elements of his original scheme, though we preserved Alan's fanciful color choice. Alan called the facade of salmon-pink brick and burgundy-tinted glass "a happy way of inviting people to come inside."

As inviting as the exterior may have been, the interior of the Crowne Plaza posed major design challenges. To accommodate the signage, Alan designed an eight-story base with 195,000 square feet of office space and 11,000 square feet of retail, as well as a health club and a convention center with a ballroom for the business travelers that an upgraded Times Square was bound to attract. To add more hotel floors—and fulfill a low-income housing requirement related to Zeckendorf Towers—we bought the Markwell, a ninety-room SRO next door on 49th Street, and transferred the air rights to our tower. I was obligated to create only forty replacement units for Union Square, but I agreed to renovate all ninety rooms at the Markwell and turn them over to a seniors' housing program run by St. Malachy's Church across 49th Street from the SRO. The Encore 49 Residence generated enough buzz to draw Mayor Ed Koch and Cardinal John Joseph O'Connor for the ribbon cutting.

The ground leases on the 48th and 49th Street corners posed another design issue: each end of the base had to function effectively as a stand-alone building with its own infrastructure so that theoretically, it could be severed from the hotel should the owner refuse to renew the ground lease. Other developers might have walked away from the site because of this drawback, but to me it was just another condition to deal with.

The signage and the stand-alone end pieces weren't the only challenges facing our architect. The entire blockfront along Broadway was earmarked for retail space, and the storefronts and signage left no room for an appropriately splashy entrance to the hotel. Alan solved the problem by running a driveway through the middle of the building and creating a dramatic two-story entry. A separate lobby on 48th Street provides access to the office base, which has a 1601 Broadway address.

In theory, the mixed-use plan was ideal. The commercial base propped up the hotel tower by seventy-five feet, giving the guest rooms better views and setting up an ongoing income source. But the office space proved hard to lease. Because of the signage, the windows were small, and stacking the hotel floors on top of the office floors compromised the layouts. Offices require wide expanses of open floor area, so building columns are generally set at twenty-five-foot intervals. Hotel rooms are designed on a tighter grid, with supporting walls spaced approximately thirteen feet apart. Marrying the two grids was an elaborate and expensive engineering feat that still didn't provide enough open space in the offices. We also decided to install the hotel swimming pool directly above the ballroom, adding another engineering challenge.

The floor layouts made leasing difficult, but we encountered an even greater obstacle. By the time we opened the Crowne Plaza in 1989, the real estate market had softened and Manhattan was flooded with office space. We finally signed a twenty-year lease with the American Management Association, a nonprofit trade organization, for the entire block of offices, though we had to sharply discount the rent.

Problems aside, the Crowne Plaza received rave reviews for the overall design, and the "light show" on the Broadway side earned us kudos for helping put the sizzle back in Times Square. Of wider importance was the social benefit: the Crowne Plaza is another example of how a development project can reclaim an area in serious decline.

World Wide Holdings, KG Land, and I bought out our other partners and operated the hotel and commercial base for a couple of years. Then I sold my shares to KG Land.

A Royal Mess

The Rihga Royal

Bill was a big idea person, but he gave a lot of time, energy, and effort to these projects. He pushed to get the best design he could. He was the first client in my experience who talked in terms of design from the inside out—how the interior space would be laid out—and he was the first to talk in terms of the quality of the design, not just the square footage.

BIRCH COFFEY, interior architect

There was a lot to love about the Rihga Royal, the city's first luxury all-suite hotel. It was well designed inside and out, with a granite base and graceful rose-brick tower that evoked classic prewar skyscraper design. When it opened in 1990, the Rihga was the tallest hotel in the city and one of the narrowest: it later won an American Concrete Institute award for the thinnest building of its height. But putting up the fifty-five-story building was a nightmare—the worst construction job of my career. Simply put, this was a case where the mob took over the job.

The project came to me through Sol Goldman. Sol owned a sliver of land running from West 54th to 55th Street, midblock between Sixth and Seventh Avenues. He wanted to build an apartment tower, but Avis had a rental-car garage on the property and refused to budge. Sol came to me in 1984 and proposed that I join him on the project. I guess he thought I might have better luck with Avis. I approached the company but also struck out. Avis had a fifty-year lease at a very low rent and no incentive to leave. I persisted, however, and after much haggling, they finally agreed to move—on the condition that we return them to the same location once our building went up.

In the interim, we had to find Avis a home. There was a garage across 54th Street, but it didn't have a license to sell gas, one of Avis's requirements. I had to negotiate with the city to secure a gas permit and then, at considerable expense, install gas pumps, storage tanks, and a car-washing facility. On top of that, the garage extracted a hefty rent from us.

Even then, we weren't cleared to build. Sol owned a small, hundred-year-old apartment building on the West 55th Street side of the property that still had a few occupants. We couldn't get a demolition permit until we emptied the building. We managed to buy out one tenant, but the other two refused our offer. Each demanded $1 million and a rent-controlled apartment—near-impossible conditions. To complicate matters, one of our holdouts was lobbying for a landmark designation for the building. It had originally been financier William Whitney's carriage house. Then in the 1920s, the upper floors were converted to studios. An artists' complex grew up around what was dubbed the Holbein Studio.

While we waited out the tenants, we went ahead with our plans. We first decided to build a high-rise with offices below and a hotel above. But when we couldn't line up a commercial tenant, we switched to a hotel with apartments on top. Then the logistics of two separate lobbies and elevator banks proved too complicated, so we focused on the hotel as the best use of the long, narrow site. We hired a consultant, Charles Bell, who suggested

we make it an all-suite hotel—a novelty in New York at the time.

The Rihga Royal Hotel (now the London NYC), New York

By then, Goldman and I had brought in two more equity partners: Ed Lewis, my hotel broker, and KG Land. None of us wanted to run a hotel, so I struck a deal with SARA, a division of a Swedish hospitality company, to operate it as part of their Royal Concordia chain. In 1986, we hired Karl Hofer as general manager and Mal Seymourian as director of marketing. Both had worked on the opening of the Helmsley Palace, a luxury hotel at 50th and Madison.

Model of the Rihga Royal Hotel

We asked Frank Williams to come up with a design. His preliminary plans called for a health club and pool at the top of the hotel, but Hofer and Seymourian recommended replacing them with meeting and banqueting rooms to draw corporate clients. Inspired by the look of traditional buildings in Paris, Frank and my son Arthur separately hit on the idea of incorporating bay windows into the design. The bay windows not only added textural interest to the facade but also gave the suites views up and down 54th Street.

We took great pains with the interior layouts. Fitting a suite into a space the size of a conventional hotel room was a major challenge, so we built a full-scale mock-up of a 550-square-foot suite on the floor below our office. Nancy helped refine the design, particularly the efficient use of space.

We broke ground in the summer of 1986, certain we would be able to empty the West 55th Street building and tear it down. But negotiations with the holdout tenants stalled, and we had to scrap plans for demolition. The rest of the 55th Street plot had already gone to a zoning-mandated through-block pedestrian walkway connecting 54th and 55th Streets, and without the missing parcel, there wouldn't be room for the side-by-side loading docks specified in Frank's plans. We'd already poured the foundation, so we were in a real bind. Fortunately, Frank was a master at navigating zoning regulations, and he and his team came up with a creative redesign, stacking one loading dock atop the other and tucking them beneath the 55th Street building.

Our troubles weren't over, however. Tishman was handling construction, budgeted at $120 million. No sooner were we out of the ground than the project quickly unraveled in a tragedy of errors. A sack of concrete fell and killed a worker. The bay windows arrived and didn't fit. Though it was the window manufacturer's error, it took us two months to resolve, which added to the mounting construction delays.

On top of all that, there was clear evidence of fraud and even mob involvement. Each month, Tishman would present us with a requisition for payment that indicated the percentage of the building completed. But when we looked at the site the discrepancies were clear. If the building was only up to, say, the fourth floor, the electrical installation couldn't possibly be 70 percent complete. At one point the plumbers decided they didn't want to finish the job, so they started filling the drainpipes with gravel. Weekly paychecks were being issued to people who weren't on the payroll: the project manager and superintendent were cashing the checks at a store around the corner and pocketing the money.

We were given completion dates that were off by six months. As the cost of overruns mounted, I demanded a budget for finishing the project. Construction stopped while we did a thorough audit to find out exactly what was left to do, how long it would take, and how much it would cost. KG Land was going to put up the money to finish the job, and I had to explain to them what was happening. Tishman admitted to having lost control of the project—momentarily, they claimed. After they fired some subcontractors and brought in new ones, they insisted that the project was back on track. Yet two months later, the situation blew up again. The fee to finish construction doubled, and in the end, the overruns cost us $25 million.

It was a disaster, and KG Land blamed us. We considered suing Tishman but decided against it. KG Land, however, went ahead with a suit. They later dropped it, but it strained our relations with Tishman when we worked together on the Ronald Reagan Building in Washington. Sol Goldman had died in 1987, but his estate filed a RICO suit against Tishman and Kumagai Gumi, KG Land's parent company, charging them with conspiracy to drive up construction costs. (RICO, the Racketeer Influenced and Corrupt Organizations Act, was initially passed to curb mob activity but has since been used widely to sue for fraud.) I was upset by the Goldman action: John Tishman and I were—and are—good friends, and I never held him responsible for what happened at the Rihga Royal; the people under him were the problem. But for me, the whole construction fiasco was more than a financial blow—it severely damaged my credibility.

Birch Coffey, interior architect

Two dining rooms at the Rihga Royal Hotel

In 1990, shortly before we were scheduled to open, the Royal Concordia hotels were taken over by Royal Hotel, a Japanese chain, which renamed the hotel the Rihga Royal. (RIHGA is an acronym for Royal International Hotel Group and Associates.) We sold our share to Rihga for $230 million but agreed to finish construction.

The new management didn't like the decor in our model rooms, so they called in Birch Coffey, an interior architect who by then had worked with us on several projects. Birch's interiors departed from the typical hotel decor. He wanted the suites to look like upscale residences, with furnishings in soft neutral colors and high-end finishes. The marble bathrooms with brass fittings were unusual for even luxury hotels at that time. The result was so elegant that I asked Birch to design the public spaces as well. Birch was well-known for his stylish steamship interiors, and he brought the same sophistication to the Rihga Royal. His lobby was spectacular, furnished with antiques and custom pieces. The dining room was equally sumptuous, with a cove ceiling lined with murals. In a smaller, private dining room, Japanese painted screens lined the walls.

The hotel was open less than a year when the Japanese chain sold it. The new owners renamed it the London NYC.

A Crowning Achievement

The Four Seasons

I think the greatest thing Bill ever did—at least in the time I worked for him—was the land assembly for the Four Seasons Hotel.

TERRY SODERBERG, former senior VP and managing director, Zeckendorf Company

As my father's house architect, I.M. Pei designed a number of projects that I was involved with in one capacity or another. But I.M. and I had never worked together on a building of mine until he designed the Four Seasons Hotel on East 57th Street in New York. Just getting to the design stage was a long and arduous process—the toughest deal of my career. Though this would prove to be a complex project for a number of reasons, the biggest challenge was assembling the building site.

I didn't have a hotel in mind in the early 1980s when I started checking out properties on the block bounded by East 57th and

Bill Zeckendorf and I.M. Pei with a model of the Four Seasons

58th Streets and Park and Madison Avenues. The parcel I ultimately put together—eleven lots totaling close to 23,000 square feet—represented years of legwork. The giant jigsaw puzzle was by far the most complicated—and expensive—land acquisition I ever undertook.

The key to a successful assemblage is to keep your intentions quiet. You don't want to tip your hand and have other developers swoop in and tie up parcels you're after. Nor do you want the owners of the lots to jack up the prices, or rent-controlled tenants to stick you up for exorbitant relocation fees. My aversion to publicity was an advantage: I could scout properties and make handshake deals before the real estate community figured out exactly what I was doing.

The block I coveted was only partially open to development. Three of the four corners were untouchable. The corner of Madison and East 57th was occupied by the Fuller Building, a forty-story Art Deco marvel housing many of the city's top art galleries. The eastern flank of the block was taken up by 470 Park, a thirteen-story prewar co-op at 58th Street, and 460 Park, a twenty-two-story metal-clad office building at 57th Street built in 1954 for the Han Sook Center, a Korean international trade organization. The rest of the block was fair game. Of particular interest to me were six brownstones along 57th Street.

While I was sizing up 57th Street, I received a call from Frank Palmer, an executive vice president of Aircoa Hospitality Services, a Denver-based hotel management firm. He was scouting around for a New York City hotel property that Aircoa could add to their portfolio. What did I think of the Blackstone Hotel—a small hotel on East 58th Street between Park and Madison? Palmer hadn't called out of the blue: he was a partner in the Eldorado Hotel, a project Nancy and I were developing in Santa Fe, New Mexico. Palmer also knew about my work in appraising and rehabilitating hotels like the Mayfair House, the Delmonico, and the McAlpin. If I felt the Blackstone had possibilities, would I be interested in coming in as Aircoa's development partner?

I knew the Blackstone. It was around the corner from our apartment, and I walked by it often. But I needed to look it over thoroughly before I would consider getting involved. Sol and Irving Goldman owned the Blackstone, but sometime in the early 1980s three commercial brokers—Alan Friedberg, Earl Reiss, and Stephen Siegel—had taken out a seventy-five-year lease on the hotel. Why they'd leased it was unclear: they'd done nothing to modernize it. I figured they were speculators, hoping to sublease the property for development rights. Meanwhile,

Assemblage for the Four Seasons

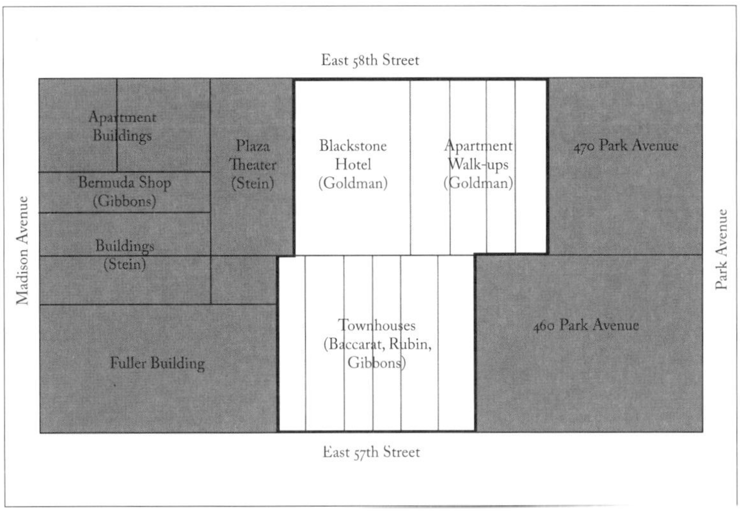

the Blackstone remained genteelly shabby, with some of its 183 rooms occupied by longtime residents protected from eviction by the city's rent-control laws.

I approached the three brokers about subleasing the hotel for six months—long enough for a thorough inspection. It took me less than two months, however, to determine that it would cost at least $12 million to upgrade the building. Even then, it would be at best a second-tier hotel, unable to compete with luxury hotels in the area like the Plaza, the Regency, the Sherry-Netherland, and the Pierre.

To be honest, I was relieved. I wasn't interested in rehabbing another hotel. My real interest in the Blackstone was as a developable site, an entree to building something significant on East 57th Street. For buildings of 100,000 square feet or more, loading docks weren't allowed on 57th Street, but if I could assemble enough property on 57th for an office tower or apartment building, I could use the Blackstone property for a service entrance and loading dock.

Enter Sir David Gibbons, a distinguished Bermudian who was chairman of his family's Butterfield Bank before serving as premier of Bermuda from 1977 to 1982. When I met him, he had turned to real estate investment, but as a side venture he ran the Bermuda Shop, a clothing boutique on Madison between 57th and 58th. He also owned four of the six townhouses on 57th Street; they were leased out at the time.

The townhouses were carryovers from the 1920s, when East 57th Street was transitioning from a tony residential address to the city's most fashionable place to shop and buy art. Fancy stores now occupied the ground floors of the houses. Understandably, given his solid-gold holdings, Sir David had every New York real estate developer in hot pursuit. But as long as he could collect premium rents, he wasn't keen on selling.

Apparently he wasn't keen on New York developers either, but Sir David and I got on well. We met a number of times, though I was careful not to push him. Then my broker, Ed Lewis, slipped me a piece of advice: the key to getting Sir David to sell would be to control the properties behind his. If we tied up access from East 58th Street, no one else would be able to develop anything on 57th because of the loading-dock restriction. We would effectively block Sir David from selling to the competition.

So I took a closer look at 58th Street. Next to the Blackstone were four apartment walk-ups, numbers 52 to 58. Like the hotel, they were owned by the Goldmans. There were twenty-two rent-controlled tenants who would have to be relocated as well as ground-floor retailers with market leases of various lengths. Ed Lewis and I sat down with Sol Goldman to negotiate. Fortunately, he was willing to give us an option for three years—enough time to empty the buildings. We made a $50,000 down payment for a six-month option, which we subsequently renewed until we bought the property in June 1988 for $17.5 million.

The commercial tenants in the storefronts moved out one by one as their leases expired, but getting the rent-controlled tenants to vacate was a laborious process. A separate agreement had to be negotiated with each one, and we had to proceed carefully. If word got out that an assemblage was in the works, it would be impossible for me to take possession. Rent-controlled tenants in such situations have all the cards in their favor, and they can—and often do—demand exorbitant fees to relocate. Worse yet, a tenant who refuses to budge can derail an entire project. Again, Edith Fisher stepped in, patiently working with the tenants one at a time. Initially we offered each tenant $25,000 to vacate, but in a few cases we had to go as high as $200,000. It took two years, but Edith finally cleared the buildings, and we took possession.

Ed Lewis's strategy worked. Once we had the properties on 58th Street, Sir David called and said he was ready to sell his townhouses. We settled on a fair price and gave him 20 percent participation in our development partnership.

The pieces were falling into place, but I needed more frontage on East 57th Street. Sir David's holdings gave us a parcel only eighty feet wide by one hundred feet deep. We would need much more than that to build anything of size. I focused on the remaining two twenty-foot brownstones, located between the Gibbons property and the Fuller Building. Baccarat, the luxury crystal dealers, owned one. The other was owned by several members of a family named Rubin; it had been leased to Pierre Cardin in the past but was empty at the time. Neither the Rubins nor Baccarat wanted to sell, though both would consider a swap: their property for a condo or suite in our new building. Since we hadn't yet built anything or even decided what to build, we couldn't make an exchange. So I came up with an alternate plan: I signed a two-hundred-year ground lease with each owner that gave me the right to raze the buildings and the owners the right to force a swap once our building went up.

The next step was to persuade Baccarat to relocate. Again we were fortunate: we were able to move them to an empty storefront on Madison just north of 58th Street until space in our new building was ready. (In the end, they didn't move into the Four Seasons but remained on Madison.)

Financing all this would require a cash infusion. Jack Shaffer, the hotel broker from Sonnenblick-Goldman who originally brought me together with Kumagai Gumi, introduced me to Peter Morris, chairman and CEO of VMS Realty Partners, a Chicago real estate investment firm. Peter was a real character, engaging and a great storyteller. Much of our meeting consisted of me listening to his considerable—and complex—marital woes. In spite of that—or perhaps because of it—it took just a few hours to convince Peter to join our development group.

With the East 57th Street properties in hand and access from 58th Street tied up, we could begin thinking seriously about what we wanted to build. I called in Frank Williams, who by then had designed a number of buildings for me. He came up with a smorgasbord of possibilities, not all of them limited to the relatively small footprint assembled so far.

Our configuration at that point wouldn't give us enough square footage for an office tower, so I continued nosing around the remaining properties on the block—without luck. Sir David wasn't interested in selling the Bermuda Shop building on

Madison. Nor could I rouse any interest from the investors who owned a small building at the corner of 58th and Madison that housed a delicatessen and twenty-eight rent-controlled apartments. I also struck out with the family of Jules Stein, the founder of MCA, who owned two nondescript buildings on Madison next to the Bermuda Shop, as well as the Plaza, a popular movie house on East 58th that had been in operation for over fifty years. The theater was originally built as the stable for Cornelius Vanderbilt II's mansion at Fifth and 57th; the small buildings on Madison had housed the Vanderbilt servants.

Efforts to enlarge the site took a turn one weekend in 1987. Nancy and I were eating a leisurely Friday night dinner at our country house in Westchester County when I received a call from Doug Stitzel, a commercial broker who had moved from New York to California. Stitzel was driving around Marin County in his Porsche, calling on his car phone. He wasted no time: why hadn't I told him about 57th Street? He claimed that for several years he'd been talking with Sir David on behalf of Bob Burns, owner of the Regent Hotels, and he was miffed that we had not only bought the 57th Street property but also controlled 58th Street.

I was pretty sure Stitzel was bluffing about his conversations with Sir David, but his call wasn't entirely a surprise. A year or so earlier, a broker friend at Edward S. Gordon had told me that Burns was interested in our assemblage. Bob was a colleague from the days when I was renovating hotel properties. I had sold the Mayfair House to him in 1978 and had tried to interest him in buying the Delmonico.

Bob Burns is creative, intelligent, and honorable—a perfect gentleman in business. Under his management the Mayfair Regent had become a favorite of the international set, and his Regent International group of hotels had few peers. By the mid-1980s there were Regent hotels in major cities throughout Asia and the Pacific; Bob was expanding into Europe and had plans to increase Regent's presence in the United States. The company was already spending $100 million to upgrade the Beverly

Wilshire Hotel, but what Bob wanted most was to build a world-class hotel in Manhattan. The Mayfair Regent wasn't quite large enough or sleek enough to fit the new corporate image and was up for sale. When Bob heard that someone was quietly buying up property along East 57th Street, he put out feelers to find out who was behind 57-57 Associates, as we were calling our partnership. Now Stitzel was hell-bent on acquiring our site for Regent International.

By that time, however, I had spent millions of dollars on land acquisition, air rights, and tenant relocation. After all that work, I wasn't anxious to sell. I said no. Stitzel pressed harder: "Then what about a joint venture?" I asked him how Bob planned to finance the project. "Money's no problem," Stitzel said. It was a mantra repeated often in the months ahead; I wish I'd been more skeptical at the time. Mr. Deep Pockets was Burns's financial partner, Harunori Takahashi, president of EIE International, a Japanese resort and hotel developer that had acquired 30 percent of Regent International. Stitzel assured me that EIE was prepared to finance the entire project, regardless of cost. "Interested now?" Stitzel asked.

It was hard not to be. Five years earlier, I'd been a limited partner with Stitzel in a rehab project in downtown San Francisco that had left us both a little poorer; now I had partners of my own to consider. Arthur Cohen held a 10 percent stake in the development of the East 57th Street site, but he was in no position to put up the $35 million we would need to complete the assemblage. I didn't have much to invest at that point, and I certainly couldn't ask our newest partner, Sir David Gibbons, to pump in money when we hadn't yet paid him for his brownstones.

I wanted to build something substantial, but nothing as grand as what Stitzel and Burns seemed to have in mind. What they envisioned would cost approximately $300 per square foot, for a total of at least $100 million—too rich even for Burns's rich patron, I assumed.

But Stitzel wouldn't take no for an answer. Throughout the ensuing summer and fall, phone calls and faxes flew back and

Will Zeckendorf, left, and Bill Zeckendorf with an associate from EIE International

forth between Stitzel in California, Burns in Hong Kong, and me in New York. Finally, in March 1988, I agreed to go to Japan for a meeting with Takahashi. My son Will and I flew to Tokyo and checked into a room on the thirtieth floor of the Imperial Hotel. We were fast asleep at 5:00 AM when we were suddenly awakened by an earthquake so strong it knocked us out of our beds. Terrifying.

We were still a bit shaken at 9:00 AM when we met with Burns and Takahashi. I told them I wasn't interested in selling the site unless the price was very high, not expecting that Takahashi would make a substantial offer. To my surprise, he repeated what Stitzel had told me: price was no object, he had access to unlimited funds, and his bank wouldn't ask him to pay it back. Takahashi wanted to build the world's tallest and most expensive hotel, he would put up the money, and he wanted us to be the developer.

With the assurance of Takahashi's millions, we headed back to New York to finish the assemblage. The three commercial brokers who held the lease on the Blackstone weren't about to relinquish their investment, which meant we couldn't buy the hotel. But our sublease didn't give us demolition rights, so I had to renegotiate the terms. Since Sol Goldman had died a few months earlier, I had to deal with his brother Irving as well as

Bill Zeckendorf with, from left, Bob Burns, Harunori Takahashi, Frank Williams, and I.M. Pei

the leaseholders. Irving proved to be a much tougher negotiator than Sol, and the three brokers were at odds with one another, so it took eight months to close a deal that would allow us to demolish the hotel. The brokers made out extremely well, receiving escalating rents starting at $1.2 million a year through 2036.

We now faced our most difficult negotiation: subleasing the Plaza Theater. The Stein family had leased it to two real estate speculators. That sent up a red flag: in all probability they were sitting on the property in order to develop it. Picking up the lease would be costly, we found out, which could make our land assemblage too expensive to proceed. But we ran the numbers and concluded that even with the theater lease, we should go ahead. Looking back, I think we paid too much for the lease, but it turned out to be a wise investment, giving us air rights to add ten floors to the hotel.

At that point, EIE was footing the bill. Takahashi paid about $150 million for the land and development rights. EIE was also financing construction and agreed to pay us a $5 million fee as project developers.

Knowing that the Japanese would require a name architect, Bob suggested I.M. Pei. I explained that we were already working with Frank Williams but offered to talk to them both. I was apprehensive about the conversation—needlessly, it turned out. Although Pei as a rule didn't collaborate, he readily agreed to work with Frank. And Frank jumped at the chance to work with I.M., whose work he greatly admired. Pei would be listed as chief architect and Frank as associate.

Sketch of the Four Seasons by architect Frank Williams

True to form, Pei insisted on complete aesthetic control of the main public spaces. We had signed up a decorator for the lobby, but when Pei saw the plan and the color scheme, he said, "I will not put my name on the building if that decorator is doing the public spaces." So he took over. Chhada Siembieda & Associates, a firm specializing in hotel interiors, designed the guest rooms.

My only demand was for an apartment in the hotel—a floor of our own, delivered as raw space. Nancy already had a set of drawings. But we later gave up the space when we discovered how prohibitively expensive it would be to build out.

At fifty-one stories, the Regent New York, as it was initially called, replaced the Rihga Royal as the tallest hotel in Manhattan and was arguably the most luxurious. Pei insisted that the entire building be faced in Magny Doré limestone—the same stone he had specified for his renovation of the Louvre. Quarried in France, it added $8 million to the total construction cost, which by the time the building was done had escalated to some $420 million—well over $1 million a room. Design features like the grand foyer with its towering thirty-three-foot ceiling made of translucent onyx and its floors of French Chassagne stone helped make the Four Seasons the most expensive hotel in the city, if not the world, when it was built.

Even the groundbreaking ceremony in September 1989 was world-class, a champagne-and-caviar reception—with dancing, no less—under a tent at the building site. Standing in front of

I.M. Pei, Nancy Zeckendorf, and Bill Zeckendorf at the Louvre, Paris

The Four Seasons, New York (opposite)

a twenty-foot-high neon sculpture of the hotel created for the occasion by artist Rudi Stern, I introduced Takahashi, the architects, and other key people on the project. There was something incongruous about the sight of all these men lined up in tuxedos and hard hats. We also had a traditional Shinto blessing ceremony—a first for any building I've been involved in.

Unbridled luxury was what Takahashi had in mind. Too bad he wasn't around to enjoy it when the hotel finally opened in June 1993. In 1991, his EIE empire collapsed, precipitating a fire sale the next year of the entire Regent International chain to the Toronto-based Four Seasons Hotels. The selling price for the chain—$122 million—was just over a quarter of what it cost to build our hotel alone. The Regent New York became the Four Seasons Hotel New York.

With the collapse of EIE, the Long-Term Credit Bank of Japan, Takahashi's lender, stepped in, and just about everyone connected with the hotel was dismissed—including us. Fortunately, by then our development work was 90 percent complete, leaving our bank-appointed successors with little to do except supervise the Tishman construction team, which couldn't easily be replaced. The Zeckendorf name was removed from the scaffolding, but the bank honored the $5 million development fee Takahashi had agreed to pay. Bob Burns, meanwhile, was forced into early retirement—with a $90 million golden parachute, it turned out, so I didn't feel too sorry for him.

Despite all the drama behind the scenes, construction of the Four Seasons proceeded largely without a hitch. Early on, we had one nasty surprise when we discovered that the foundation of the apartment building next door to the Blackstone was encroaching on that hotel's basement. We had planned to install the Four Seasons kitchen in the basement and the restaurant on the lobby level, but without the Blackstone basement space we had to move the kitchen up.

The two architects, Pei and Williams, worked together seamlessly, their strengths and personalities complementary. Terry Soderberg, our project manager on the job, remembers one incident:

57th Street facade of the Four Seasons (opposite)

> Frank Williams had done these beautiful pen-and-ink drawings—floor plans and elevations of the public rooms on the main floor. He was pointing out things on the drawings to Pei, when all of a sudden I started shaking my head. Pei turned to me and said, "Sonny, what's wrong?" I said, "Mr. Pei, there's an eight-foot difference between the elevation on 57th Street and the elevation on 58th. If you build according to these plans, you'll end up with an eight-foot gap in the middle of the lobby where the walls and the floor don't line up." Frank froze and said, "Uh-oh," expecting the worst from Pei, I suppose. But all Pei said was, "Good point." Then he pulled out a big black marker and in bold, sweeping strokes sketched a flight of stairs on Frank's beautiful drawing. A few minutes later, Pei thrust the drawing at me and asked, "How's that?" "Fine," I told him. Everyone smiled. Problem solved.

Frank Williams, who was already on his way to earning worldwide recognition, later described collaborating with Pei as "an unparalleled working experience." The two remained fast friends until Frank's death in 2010 at age seventy-three.

The building they created is a masterpiece, visually arresting from both the 57th and 58th Street sides, but the main entrance is particularly striking. The monumental ninety-foot-high limestone base is punched with a huge oculus, and from there the tower rises in a series of setbacks crowned by custom-designed lanterns that give off a festive glow at night. Though distinctly of our time, the building follows in the tradition of classic New York masonry skyscrapers, a handsome counterpoint to its Art Deco neighbor, the Fuller Building.

Paul Goldberger, architecture critic for the *New York Times*, gave the Four Seasons a thumbs up, despite the somewhat ambivalent headline on his review: "A Grand Hotel, But Not What You'd Call Homey." Indeed, more accurate descriptors would be *imposing, monumental, opulent.* According to Goldberger, the building's most notable characteristic is its "staggering grandeur."

Moving On

My mission as a real estate developer was to create properties that made the city a safer, more comfortable, more aesthetically pleasing place to live. For much of the 1980s, the Zeckendorf Company was flying high, with projects worth over $3 billion. Between 1980 and 1991, we built thirty buildings. And we were a full-service organization, not merely developing our own properties as a managing partner with equity but also offering our expertise as project managers.

Between New York and Santa Fe, I had more than a dozen projects in the works when the stock market crashed in 1987. I was leveraged to the hilt, and it was only a matter of time before I ran aground.

The early 1990s were not kind to developers, and I was no exception. With my son Will's help, I set about restructuring the financing on problematic projects and took steps to pay down my debt. I'm proud to say that unlike many other developers, I was never forced into bankruptcy. But I did see my portfolio trimmed to almost nothing as I fought to keep the company alive through the market slump and a run of personal bad luck. As part of my reordering, I shifted the company toward property management and leasing, forming Zeckendorf Realty with my sons.

My last big deal in New York was assembling the parcels and air rights on Park Avenue and East 60th Street that my sons, Will and Arthur, ultimately parlayed into 515 Park, the most successful new luxury condominium of the 1990s. It took me years of intense negotiations to put that site together, and I consider it my legacy to the boys. By then, they had worked alongside me for well over a decade: that on-the-job training was also a bequest to them, just as working with my father had been his bequest to me.

As the 1990s rolled on, financial setbacks and worsening health took their toll. After years of back injuries and surgeries, I could barely move. Financially, I was struggling but holding my own. Then several longstanding business partners turned against me, and an especially ugly incident with one of them knocked the fight out of me. Together, these events provided the impetus to retire to Santa Fe, a place with special meaning for Nancy and me.

In close to fifty years in the development business, I had never encountered the viciousness that cast a shadow over my final years in New York. But if there was any good to come of that time, it was finding out just how many loyal friends and associates I had. Their kindness and support carried me through.

515 Park

Legacy to My Sons

[My father] taught us everything we know. He left us with an extraordinary education and value base. The level of knowledge, the hard-won business experience, the ability to figure out opportunities and make the best use of them—we would never have received this training anywhere else.

WILL ZECKENDORF, *New York Sun*, July 18, 2006

If the Four Seasons assemblage, with its eleven separate parcels, was the most complex I ever put together, 515 Park ran a close second. Five parcels made up the site, and there wasn't a straightforward acquisition in the bunch. Ultimately, the deal involved a checkerboard of land acquisitions, air rights, and zoning regulations; negotiations with a nonprofit, an estate, and a reluctant seller; an attempted takeover by hostile competitors; and partners and financing that came and went. It took nearly a decade to complete, but in the end, it all worked out.

515 Park Avenue, New York

The condominium at 515 Park Avenue marked a seismic shift in residential development. It was the first truly luxe apartment house to go up on Park in decades, and the units sold at record prices, raising the bar on luxury housing in New York from then on. I assembled the site, then my sons, Will and Arthur, went on to complete the deal and put up the building. It was my last project in New York, and bringing it to the table was my way of passing the torch to my sons.

In 1987 I received a call from George Klein, another New York developer. He asked if we'd be interested in purchasing a building at 515 Park Avenue as a joint venture. I had never done business with Klein, though within a year we were competing for the Ronald Reagan Building in Washington, but he was a successful commercial developer with a good reputation. We had the residential development experience he was after. The proposed location was ideal—the corner of Park Avenue and East 60th Street, a block west of Bloomingdale's and the 59th Street subway hub. Best of all, the twelve-story building on the lot was vacant: there would be no residents to relocate or buy out.

Built as a co-op apartment house in 1912, 515 Park had been converted to offices for several Zionist organizations in 1958. There was talk it had been the New York headquarters of the Mossad, Israel's intelligence service, and that somewhere in the building were detention and interrogation facilities. If there were any, we never found them.

We discussed various possibilities for developing 515. George wanted to renovate the existing 72,000-square-foot building, adding as many floors as possible, for an apartment house or office tower. We rejected this plan right away: the building wasn't strong enough to support more than four additional floors, and we would need to go higher for the economics to work. The alternative was to demolish the building and erect a new one. But that, too, was problematic: the lot extended only one hundred feet along Park Avenue and sixty feet along 60th Street, too small for a building of substantial size. That left us with a third option: to expand the site.

In early 1989 George and I each put up $400,000 to buy 515 within a year. No sooner had we signed the agreement than George got cold feet, and when a Brazilian bank offered to buy 515 at a $400,000 profit, he wanted to sell. I didn't. Tobishima, a Japanese construction company we had brought in as an equity partner, agreed to buy out George and finance a larger building that would include surrounding properties. George, however, was angry with me for costing him the profit from the Brazilian bank. We closed on the Park Avenue property in September 1990, with Tobishima putting up $38 million.

From a zoning standpoint, 515 Park was an anomaly. It was considered part of the commercial zone south of 60th Street, where we would be allowed to put up a building with an FAR of 15, or 90,000 square feet, fifteen times the square footage of our site. However, the portion of the property along East 60th Street was landmarked and zoned for residential use, limiting the height of the building to sixteen floors. Buying up the four adjacent properties along East 60th Street would give us development rights totaling more than 200,000 square feet, allowing us to build much higher.

Acquiring the 60th Street properties was easier said than done. At 108 East 60th, a twenty-foot brownstone two doors east of 515, I was able to buy the fee simple, an unrestricted deed that would give us demolition rights. However, at 106 East 60th, the twenty-foot brownstone right next door to our property, I wasn't as successful: the owner refused to sell anything but air rights. We negotiated for close to a year, finally settling on a price of $8 million. That was outrageously high, but we needed the air rights to go beyond the limitations of our site.

The property east of 108, at 110 East 60th Street, which extended through the block to 59th Street, was owned by the Lighthouse, a nonprofit known until 1989 as the New York Association for the Blind. They were getting ready to demolish their building and put up a new headquarters on the site. I persuaded them to move their new building twenty feet east to accommodate us. For the Lighthouse to be able to move, however, I would need to buy the small building to their east, at 112 East 60th Street. It was owned by the estate of Sol Goldman. I'd done a number of deals with Sol and Irving Goldman and had partnered with Sol on the Rihga Royal Hotel just before he died. But buying their building proved to be a challenge, since the commercial tenant on the ground floor wouldn't move. I finally got a commitment for the air rights.

At that point, we owned 515 Park and 108 East 60th, had acquired the air rights of 106 East 60th, and had verbal agreements from the Lighthouse and the Goldman estate. But the Lighthouse couldn't wait any longer to begin work on the new headquarters. They went ahead and built on the existing property, and we made a deal to buy their unused development rights. Their 10,000 square feet of air rights were critical to us for what is known as a "zoning lot merger"—joining two or more adjacent properties into a single lot for zoning purposes, which allows unused development rights from one to be transferred to the other. A residential building in a commercial district is allowed an FAR of only 12, but an office building on the same lot would be allowed to build fifteen times the square footage of the lot. The Lighthouse was commercially zoned, so including them in our zoning lot would give us an FAR of 15.

At that point, we decided to go ahead and have our architect, Frank Williams, draw up preliminary plans. Because we had only air rights to 106, Frank designed a tall, very narrow tower—a sliver building—fronting on Park Avenue on the original 515 footprint.

Just as our assemblage was coming together nicely, the Japanese real estate market collapsed, and Tobishima was forced to freeze the project. We lost our deposits on both the Lighthouse and Goldman properties, and were left with a $50 million mortgage that grew to $70 million over the next eight years—and an unbuildable site.

The next few years were the worst of my career. Everything ground to a halt. Everything, that is, but my financial situation—and my health. I lost nearly everything to my creditors, and as my financial situation worsened, so did my health. Years of horseback riding caught up with me, leaving me with crippling back pain and a round of surgeries and complications from which I've never fully recovered.

I owed Chemical Bank about $10 million, and the bank was calling for more collateral. To satisfy them, I pledged my interest in 515, along with other properties. To my shock Victor Elmaleh and Frank Stanton of World Wide Holdings—my partners for much of the preceding decade—chose that moment to turn against me. When Chemical foreclosed on my collateral and decided to sell my debt, including my stake in 515, Victor and Frank bought the note at a discounted price and filed a judgment against me. I had lengthy discussions with them about buying back 515 and some of my other assets. For a while I even thought they might invest in 515 as a joint venture. Instead they took a hardline position that seemed to be aimed at putting me out of business.

This was a terrible blow. I felt betrayed by the partners I'd worked with on some of the biggest deals of my career. I'd been counting on 515 to put me back in the game once I was on solid footing with the bank and my investors, and seeing it slip away was agony. I finally worked out an agreement giving World Wide virtually everything I had left, including my interest in Worldwide Plaza, in exchange for an arrangement that would allow me to keep 515. Victor and Frank gave me a $350,000 credit for my small stake in Worldwide Plaza and offered me six months to pay off another $500,000.

During one of our settlement discussions, Victor and Frank found out that we hadn't yet signed the option with the Lighthouse. They immediately went to one of the Lighthouse trustees and offered to top our price, saying that the organization shouldn't be dealing with me anyway, since World Wide Holdings now controlled my interests. In response, we raised our payment to the Lighthouse to $2 million, putting 515 back on line. But World Wide's lien on my assets made it virtually impossible for me to take further action on the project.

Claims on 515 then began to pour in from unexpected quarters. I received a call from Jules Demchick, a New York developer I hardly knew. He had gone to Alvin Dworman—a banker holding my $3 million guarantee on Soundview Estates, a disastrous World Wide project for low-cost housing in the Bronx—and had purchased the guarantee, along with the mortgage on the project. Demchick wanted to take over 515 and offered us $1.5 to $2 million to "clear out of the way." In view of all that was happening, we briefly considered his offer. But I still felt that 515 would be my last chance to make a statement in New York, and we turned Demchick down.

By 1995, the residential real estate market was on the upswing. My sons, who had gone out on their own in 1992, saw a growing market for large, luxury apartments and took over development of 515. I was out of the project financially by then, but I stayed on as a consultant to complete the assemblage.

Mitsubishi Trust and Banking Corporation was holding the mortgage on 515 with a guarantee from Tobishima, and it seemed clear that the only way the deal would make economic sense would be to buy the mortgage. Demchick nearly beat us to it, going to Mitsubishi and telling them that I could no longer exercise the option on 515 Park because he had control over it. Once again, it looked as if we might lose 515. Then Will and Arthur brought in Goldman Sachs's Whitehall Real Estate Fund as an equity partner. The project was back on track.

We still had to buy the mortgage on 515 from Mitsubishi, however. I heard that Demchick had teamed up with Donald Trump, presumably to buy the mortgage. I made the mistake of phoning a friend at Goldman Sachs to find out what Trump was up to. My friend called back a few days later and said, "That was the stupidest phone call you've ever made. As soon as I talked to Trump, he decided he wanted to buy 515 and asked me to be his broker."

It finally came down to a bidding war. The original offer was $34 million. Demchick got it up to $38 million. Then Mitsubishi decided to arrange a telephone auction between the Demchick group and the Zeckendorf-Goldman group. We had a major advantage over Demchick: Tobishima and I had taken out the option on the Lighthouse air rights under a separate partnership. No one could build a residential tower of any size without those rights. We also owned the fee simple on 108 and the air rights on 106. So anyone buying the mortgage on 515 would have

Bill Zeckendorf with Will, Arthur, and two associates at the groundbreaking for 515 Park Avenue

to deal with me, as well as find a way to get the air rights from the Lighthouse.

Demchick bid up the auction to $42.5 million and then dropped out. He must have realized that it would cost him at least another $2 or $3 million to buy us out. By then, the Lighthouse had finished their new building, so we concluded the deal for their unused development rights, which allowed an additional eleven stories at 515.

Frank Williams's final design was a slender forty-three-story tower that at the time was the tallest residential building on Park Avenue. Inspired by the classic apartment buildings of the 1920s, 515 is clad in Magny Doré limestone and beige brick, with setbacks on the fifteenth, thirty-third, and forty-third floors. Many of the thirty-eight apartments have spectacular views up and down Park Avenue and across Central Park. From the top floors the panorama stretches as far as the George Washington Bridge. The residences contain all the trappings of traditional upper-crust dwellings—thirty-foot living rooms, formal dining rooms, libraries, fireplaces, high ceilings, servants' quarters—along with thoroughly modern conveniences like media rooms, climate-controlled wine cellars, and gourmet kitchens with Poggenpohl appliances.

At the time of the groundbreaking in May 1998, few believed 515 would succeed. The location was too far down Park to attract upscale buyers, critics said, and the prices, starting at $1,500 a square foot—$400 above the going rate—were way too high. Happily for us, the critics were wrong on both counts. By the end of 1999, all but two of the apartments had sold for from $2,000 a square foot to as much as $3,000, the highest prices for any New York apartments up to that point.

I had no equity in 515, so I reaped none of the financial rewards. My sons, however, did well, and 515 Park launched them on the spectacular careers they have today, as New York's leading developers of luxury residential buildings.

For me, the saga of 515 is bittersweet. My role in putting together the assemblage is largely forgotten, but I can still take satisfaction in the building's success. From a developer's standpoint, the project is a textbook case in how to use air rights creatively to more than quadruple the buildable square footage of a small site and achieve its full value.

Leaving New York

It should be emphasized how universally Bill is loved and admired. Real estate is a field that attracts tough, hard, shrewd people, but Bill is widely respected as a person of character and competence. He regards his handshake as binding.

DANIEL ROSE, real estate developer and lifelong friend

Nobody likes to dwell on setbacks and failures, but they're the downside of the risk-and-reward stakes of real estate development. The market collapse in the late 1980s and early 1990s hit me hard. My creditors—including, sadly, onetime partners—blocked me from participating in deals like 515 Park that would have enabled me to settle my debts and get back on top.

Caught in the downturn, several of my largest projects were repossessed after commercial tenants fell on hard times. At Zeckendorf Towers, hailed for catalyzing the turnaround of Union Square, the sole tenant of the retail base, Integrated Resources, went bankrupt before we'd even received their first rent check. When we failed to fill the space, which had been fitted out expressly for Integrated, we couldn't pay the interest on our loan and lost the property to our lender, Equitable Life.

A similar situation cost us 4 Columbus Circle, an office building adjacent to Central Park Place. The architecture firm of Swanke Hayden Connell had designed the seven-story building to their specifications, reserving the top four floors and the penthouse for themselves. But as commissions evaporated during the building slump, they were forced to downsize and move out. Chemical Bank, which had just merged with our lender, Manufacturers Hanover, refused to renegotiate our loan and took over the building instead. Chemical later sold the building to Steelcase.

Worldwide Plaza, the mixed-use complex lauded for opening up Eighth Avenue and Midtown West to blue-chip corporations, suffered several blows. After the ad agency N. W. Ayer, one of our largest tenants, lost their biggest account, they defaulted on the rent and had to move out, leaving six empty floors we couldn't fill. At the other end of the property, blocks of condominiums remained unsold, casualties of a sluggish residential market and lingering questions about the neighborhood. Unwilling to ride out the storm, our lender, Deutsche Bank, sold the mortgage to the Blackstone Group at a $150 million loss.

I fell victim to some other deals that soured, including a disastrous affordable-housing development in the Bronx called Shorehaven. Unless a developer has very deep pockets or a large portfolio of properties, leverage is the only way to finance a deal. I seldom financed a project alone. Having multiple partners allowed me to share the risk, but it also meant sharing the returns. And often it meant taking my money out in order to invest it in my next venture before I could reap the profits.

It's ironic that while all this was happening, I was one of four people named to the 1989 *Crain's New York Business* All-Star Team. In its April 9, 1990, issue, *Crain's* called us "a diverse group of executives who share in common one uncommon trait: They have been willing to do the unexpected, even the controversial." Despite the timing, I appreciated *Crain's* endorsement:

> William Zeckendorf, Jr. illustrates what sets the *Crain's* all-stars apart. In an age when developing in New York City is considered a troublesome venture fraught with bureaucratic delays and confrontations with community groups, Mr. Zeckendorf gets important projects done on schedule, elegantly, and profitably. He has managed to work well with interests as diverse as neighborhood activists and Japanese investors, and his foresight has led him to build projects that are transforming two marginal neighborhoods.

I learned the hard way how unyielding some partners could be. I was probably too trusting, assuming that my partners would act honorably except in rare instances. Unfortunately, as the market softened, "rare instances" came up too often. I fell afoul of personal guarantees, which I'd always tried to avoid, and found myself in the unenviable position of not being able to cover my debts. I lost pretty much everything as a result.

I had given my longtime partners Victor Elmaleh and Frank Stanton of World Wide Holdings a personal guarantee of $3.3 million on two Gimbels deals that were ultimately disasters. By 1999 the debt, with interest, was close to $6.5 million. Victor and Frank assured me they wanted to work out a friendly repayment plan, and I was prepared to believe them. After all, we'd been in business together for more than fifteen years. But somewhere along the line they changed their minds.

By then, I was spending most of my time in Santa Fe, where Nancy and I had a condo, and I'd been working on several development projects. One day in July 1999, I received a call from the front desk of the Hotel Delmonico in New York telling me that several people—including a lawyer, a locksmith, and a city marshal—were requesting access to our apartment. The front desk did not have our keys, so the city marshal produced a warrant giving them the right to enter the apartment any way they could. It turned out that the marshal was executing a court order orchestrated by Victor Elmaleh. I quickly phoned my lawyer

Bill and Nancy Zeckendorf's house in Chappaqua, New York, with addition by Frank Williams

and discovered that by some curious twist, the break-in was legal. The warrant claimed that there was a safe in our apartment that was hotel property and that the marshal had the right to enter the premises to examine the contents of the safe. Victor was searching for assets to seize in payment of my debt to World Wide, and he expected to find a safe full of valuables. But there was no safe, and there were no valuables.

It was bad enough that they had forced their way into our apartment. Even worse, they had brought with them a reporter for the *Wall Street Journal.* On March 21, 2000, the *Journal* printed a front-page story about the break-in that was riddled with inaccuracies and rife with baseless charges. "Zeckendorf's Real-Estate Empire Unravels as Creditors Close In" screamed the headline—more appropriate to a gossipy tabloid than to one of the nation's most respected dailies.

I was so hurt and humiliated by the article that I decided not to return to New York. I couldn't face anyone, not even my family or closest friends. All these years later, I can still feel the sting, the sense of betrayal and loss. To have a colleague turn on me so viciously, apparently to frighten and humiliate me, was beyond my comprehension.

That's when I learned what true support is. From the moment the *Journal* article hit the newsstands, letters, emails, cards, and calls poured in. Each was a graceful and generous expression of kindness, sympathy, and warmth. My business partner's cruelty was no match for the decency of others. I never knew I had so many friends. I even heard from people I'd never met, conveying their outrage at the *Journal* article and the bullying tactics it described. I offered to resign from every board I was serving on, but all of them begged me to stay.

In retrospect, not every word in the *Journal* article was venal or false. Buried in the text was one complimentary paragraph:

> Among the elite of New York's 1980s real-estate society, Mr. Zeckendorf, in his quiet and dignified way, stood out. With his elegant ballerina wife Nancy at his side, he seemed appealingly unpretentious, particularly next to some of the publicity-craving operators who became big news in the '80s building frenzy.

Nice, yes, but faint praise after the damning words in the rest of the article. No doubt the break-in and news story were so devastating to me because they evoked memories of the breakup of my father's company, Webb & Knapp, fifty years earlier, and his personal bankruptcy—events that dampened his natural good spirits and sidelined him from the development game he so dearly loved. After picking up the pieces following the demise of Webb & Knapp, I was determined never to follow in those particular footsteps of my father's. It was especially galling to find myself accused of being in the same straits.

I'm a firm believer, however, that just about any problem has a solution. Resolving it may take time—sometimes more time than an impatient lender is willing to extend. That's unfortunate. Unlike a number of developers, I never sidestepped my obligations by declaring bankruptcy. I took steps to pay down my debt. If I lost face momentarily, I never lost my good name. But in any business, not just in real estate, there's always a wild card—vindictiveness. Some people are just out to get you. That's something I'll never understand. I've experienced enough pain in my own life not to willingly inflict it on others.

Santa Fe: New Beginnings

I never expected to end up in the Southwest. I'm a New Yorker born and bred. And with the exception of the Ronald Reagan Building in Washington, for most of my career all my major development projects were in New York City.

But in the early 1980s, I was offered a piece of land in Santa Fe, New Mexico. The luxury condo development I built—Los Miradores—was a financial disaster at first, but with time the condo idea caught on, and the complex became one of the area's most successful. As often happens, one thing led to another, and over the decade after Los Miradores, Nancy and I developed four more projects in Santa Fe. That set the stage for settling here permanently in the early 1990s.

Moving to Santa Fe was a homecoming of sorts, though it was not until we started work on Los Miradores that I discovered I had roots in the Southwest dating back to the nineteenth century. My great-grandfather William Zeckendorf followed his two older brothers to America from Germany in 1856, then crossed the country to Santa Fe.

My ancestors were smart businessmen—merchants who established stores in New Mexico and Arizona—with a strong pioneering gene that my father and I seem to have inherited. But my great-grandfather William also passed on a real estate gene. That may explain why my father and I were far more interested in the buildings than in any merchandise inside.

After Los Miradores, I developed Sierra del Norte, the high-end subdivision where Nancy and I now live. I also built the town's first four-star hotel, the Eldorado, and the smaller Hotel Santa Fe. Our most unusual—and most satisfying—project was the Lensic Performing Arts Center. We refurbished a 1930s-era movie house, transforming a beloved local landmark into a twenty-first-century theater that is a hub of Santa Fe's cultural life.

My partner in all these ventures has been my wife, Nancy. She has loved New Mexico since her days as a ballet dancer in the 1960s, when she danced with the Santa Fe Opera. In New York, I often relied on Nancy's impeccable taste and organizational skills, but in Santa Fe she came into her own as a developer, proving she's as astute at project management as she is at design.

My affection for Santa Fe was slower to emerge than Nancy's, but the southwestern city is now home. Here, I've been able to do what I like best, and my profitable ventures have allowed me to repay my debts.

In recent years, my health has slowed me down. My years of horseback riding and a serious fall took a toll on my back, and I've been through half a dozen or more surgeries. I'm no longer as mobile as I used to be—I'm on a walker for my back and oxygen for chronic obstructive pulmonary disease, or COPD. But for most of the past two decades, I've been busy non-stop with development projects and community service in Santa Fe. Nancy and I have immersed ourselves in local causes, happy to lend our expertise to arts organizations, educational institutions, and health care facilities. Our life out here is every bit as rewarding as the one we led in New York, if somewhat slower paced. I say *somewhat* because we've never really retired. I don't think either of us knows what the word means.

The Zeckendorfs in the Southwest

Return to My Roots

The Zeckendorfs showed agility in adjusting quickly to new conditions. They were "movers" and they were "joiners."

FLOYD S. FIERMAN, *Guts And Ruts: The Jewish Pioneer in the American Southwest*

I don't remember hearing much about my family's past as I was growing up: my father was too busy living in the present. But I often accompanied him on business trips out West. One of those trips took us to Los Angeles for the opening of Century City, my father's development on the old 20th Century Fox back lot. For some reason—to honor Dad, I suppose—Spyros Skouras, the head of Fox, built a replica of the original William Zeckendorf store in Tucson, Arizona, as part of the opening celebration. There's a photo of my father and me, standing on the porch of the mocked-up general store, grinning ear to ear.

My Zeckendorf forebears were among the pioneering German Jewish immigrants who settled in the American South-

The first William Zeckendorf, 1875

west in the mid-nineteenth century. My great-grandfather, the first William Zeckendorf, was only fourteen when he arrived in New York from Hanover, Germany, in November 1856. In *Zeckendorfs and Steinfelds: Merchant Princes of the American Southwest,* my cousin Bettina O'Neil Lyons chronicles the fortunes of my enterprising forebears as ambition drew them westward in pursuit of a better life. As Tina tells it, William stayed in the East for six months to attend school, then boarded a wagon train for the three-month trip to Santa Fe. He went to work for his older brothers, Aaron and Louis, who had arrived before him and had opened a store, later adding a second one in Albuquerque, and eventually settling permanently in Tucson, Arizona.

I'm a history buff, a voracious reader, particularly of American history. Perhaps I come by that interest naturally. Aaron Zeckendorf cofounded the Santa Fe Historical Society in February 1860, and my great-grandfather joined the group a few months later. Cousin Tina writes that William donated a few items to the society: a half-cent coin, an elk horn whip he bought from an Apache Indian, and what are described only as "numerous historical papers." Tina doesn't say what the papers were or where he got them, and as far as I know they're not on display at the historical society today, although it's possible they're stashed away in the archives.

New Mexico was still a U.S. territory when my ancestors arrived; it didn't become a state until 1912. But Santa Fe was no sleepy village. It was a thriving town with a substantial international community. William Zeckendorf reportedly spoke German, English, French, and "prayerbook Hebrew."

When the Civil War broke out, the Union Army recruited New Mexicans. William, nineteen by then, volunteered and was assigned to the First New Mexico Volunteer Infantry Regiment, as assistant quartermaster under Kit Carson. Later my great-grandfather claimed he'd been captured by Confederate forces, then released a year later in a prisoner exchange. My ears pricked up when I heard that, since I was an army observer at two pris-

Bill and his father on the porch of a replica of the original William Zeckendorf general store, 1963

oner exchanges during the Korean War. But cousin Tina suggests that William was probably exaggerating his capture for effect: "He was not above self-aggrandizement," she writes.

During the Civil War, A. & L. Zeckendorf & Co. was a major supplier to Union troops, securing a number of lucrative government contracts, and the store continued to supply frontier outposts for some time thereafter. But the war years were bad for business in other ways. When Confederate soldiers overran Santa Fe, Aaron and Louis closed their store and moved the stock to Albuquerque. After the war ended in 1865, they reopened in Santa Fe, in a larger space on the Plaza—the city's central square and marketplace—selling everything from clothes and dry goods to groceries and liquor. The *New Mexican* touted the new location as "by far the most commodious and elegant building in New Mexico, and we doubt if it has its equal west of the Missouri River." Even then, the Zeckendorfs gravitated toward aesthetically pleasing real estate.

The new store was so successful that soon the shelves were bare. When a shipment of replacement stock was lost in a snowdrift, Aaron and Louis were forced to close. That ended the Zeckendorf presence in Santa Fe until Nancy and I arrived more than a century later.

But the two brothers, canny businessmen, discovered an underserved market in the Arizona Territory. They loaded up twelve wagons of goods and headed for Tucson. After selling out their stock, they went back to Albuquerque, loaded up sixteen more wagons, and returned to Arizona. This time, the goods were slower to move, so they opened a store. Younger brother William was charged with picking up merchandise shipped from New York to Albuquerque and transporting it to Tucson. The wagon trains had to go through Apache country, so William hired Apache escorts to protect the goods. Later, when the Apaches started attacking travelers and raiding outlying settlements, William—ever the adventurer—joined in various efforts to subdue the Indians, on one occasion helping a group of Mexicans track down the raiders who had stolen their cattle.

William lived behind the store and served as head of security, firing his shotgun to scare off burglars. One time he wasn't quick enough, and thieves made off with three kegs of butter—the whiskey barrels wouldn't fit through the window.

My great-grandfather—"Will" to his brothers and "Z" to everyone else—earned a reputation as a colorful character with a fondness for staging fireworks displays on just about any occasion. In 1870, when Aaron and Louis closed the store in Albuquerque, it was William who brokered the deal to buy the new store in Tucson. By then, my great-grandfather had amassed real estate worth $4,000 and personal worth of $120,000—$1.8 million in today's dollars. He had also snagged a government contract to carry the mail but managed to anger everyone by failing to deliver it. Put in charge of A. & L. Zeckendorf by his brothers, William worked his way back into favor by remodeling the store and filling it with what the local paper described as "one of the grandest assortments of goods ever brought to this section of the Territory."

My great-grandfather's enthusiasm for shopkeeping was short-lived, however. His talents and focus lay elsewhere. As cousin Tina explains, "William had far more interest and expertise in playing games of chance and being Tucson's irrepressible Z than in managing a business."

By then, the Zeckendorf interests extended well beyond retail to real estate, transportation, and mining. With William no longer minding the store, Louis, who had moved to New York, was forced to return to Tucson to help put the family business in order. Then in 1872, while visiting Santa Fe, Aaron died unexpectedly at age thirty-seven. Unable to find a buyer for the company, Louis had no choice but to sell it to William and their brother-in-law, Theodore Welisch. William and Theodore bought up several city blocks in Tucson, presumably intending to build bigger, better premises. But before they could develop the property, the two fell out. Welisch sued William for neglecting the company; William countersued and bought out Welisch. Reluctantly, Louis went back into business with William, leaving my great-grandfather in charge of the renamed Zeckendorf Bros. while Louis returned to New York.

Even then, Louis couldn't get William to knuckle down. The "irrepressible Z" turned operations over to a minion and dove into more exciting pursuits, namely mining and politics. My father never had any political aspirations, but I recognized something of Dad in Tina's description of William: "an affable, outgoing man who enjoyed being in the community and getting involved in any activity that would draw attention to himself." My great-grandfather failed in his first bid for public office,

William and Julia Frank Zeckendorf, c. 1900

Zeckendorf & Staab, Tucson

but in 1875 he was elected to the Legislative Assembly of the Territory of Arizona.

Louis's efforts to domesticate his brother were as futile as his attempts to get William to be more responsible in business. But on a trip to New York in 1875 William met a lovely young woman, Julia Frank, and surprised everyone by marrying her that fall. My father, in his autobiography, describes the moment on their honeymoon when Julia discovered her husband's true colors as a "deep-dyed frontiersman": "He arrived at breakfast with a pistol on each hip, crisscrossed bandoliers of ammunition across his chest, and a rifle in his hand." William was probably laying it on thick to impress his audience. No word on his bride's reaction.

Just as Louis had hoped, marriage seemed to have calmed William. Two daughters were born in quick succession, followed by my grandfather Arthur William Zeckendorf in 1880. By then, William had left Zeckendorf Bros., his partnership with Louis, intending to relocate to New York. But his father-in-law had other ideas and urged my great-grandfather to reconsider. William and his old friend Zadoc Staab opened Zeckendorf & Staab, a store in Tucson. Louis, meanwhile, renamed his store L. Zeckendorf & Co. and brought in his nephew Albert Steinfeld, his sister Julia's son, as his partner. Louis and Albert remained partners until 1904, when Albert bought out his uncle and established Albert Steinfeld & Co. By the time I attended the University of Arizona in the 1950s, Steinfeld's, owned by my uncle Harold, was the biggest and best department store in Tucson. In 1954, my father took part in a gala celebration of the hundredth anniversary of the enterprise my Zeckendorf ancestors had established back in Santa Fe.

The arrival of the railroad in 1880 brought goods directly to Tucson, ending the wagon-train supply chain central to the pioneer economy. William and Staab broke up their partnership, and my great-grandfather tried to bring a second railroad line to Tucson. After his efforts were unsuccessful, he opened a branch of his store in Tombstone, Arizona, then a prosperous mining town.

All seemed to be going well for William until 1883, when to everyone's surprise, his business failed. In an eerie preview of my father's fate, the company's assets went to William's creditors, and in 1885, he declared bankruptcy. His plan was to open another store, however, and just as my stepmother Marion gave my father the money to start up again, Julia's parents bankrolled my great-grandfather's new enterprise, J. Frank & Co.

Julia Zeckendorf had a civilizing effect on William, but she was homesick for New York, and in 1891 William moved his family east, turning J. Frank & Co. over to a manager. Like his previous store, this one failed, and in 1893 William left Tucson for good, his creditors in pursuit.

The Zeckendorfs lived first on West 116th Street in Manhattan, then moved to Far Rockaway, Queens. My grandfather Arthur went into the shoe business and married Byrd Rosenfield from Paris, Illinois, which is where my father, William Zeckendorf Sr., was born in 1905. The following year, great-grandfather William died of cancer at age sixty-four.

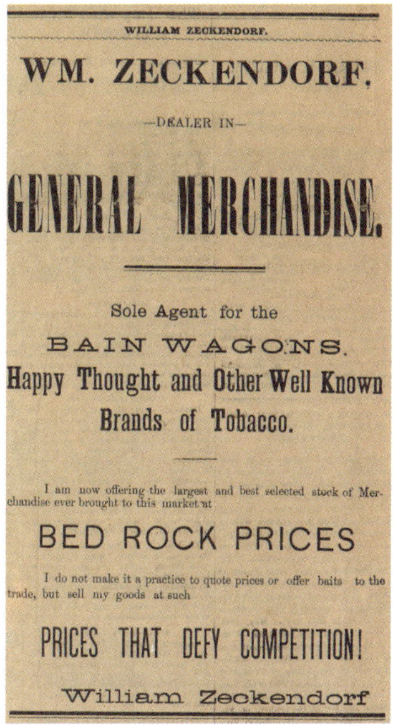

Newspaper ad for William Zeckendorf's general store

Nancy Zeckendorf

A Living Treasure

The current Santa Fe Opera house is world famous, in no small part because of Bill and Nancy. I remember sitting with them and John Crosby on the patio at the Opera Ranch, discussing John's vision of a new, expanded theater with a roof. John's commitment was the catalyst that got the redesign going, and Bill was very helpful behind the scenes, advising John. But it was Nancy's leadership and fund-raising that made it happen.

DAVID ATER, development partner

Santa Fe isn't just my ancestral home: it's also where I met my wife, Nancy—indirectly, at least. In 1962, my mother and stepfather, the music critic Irving Kolodin, were staying in Santa Fe while he covered the opera season for the *Saturday Review of Literature.* The dancer and actress Vera Zorina, who had the lead in Stravinsky's opera *Persephone,* invited my mother and Irving for lunch at Bishop's Lodge, the resort where Zorina was staying. Among the other guests that day were four young dancers

Nancy Zeckendorf (née King) in production of *Carmen* (left)

Nancy in *Don Quixote*

who were appearing with the opera. One of them, a pretty ballerina named Nancy King, was seated at my mother's table.

A principal dancer with the Metropolitan Opera Ballet, Nancy was spending her second summer in Santa Fe. Her prodigious talent had taken her from tiny Tidioute, Pennsylvania, to a coveted spot at the Juilliard School in New York, and from there to the Met in 1954. Her credits also include Broadway, summer stock, and the European touring company of *Oklahoma*. She even appeared on *The Ed Sullivan Show* in a novel restaging of *Rigoletto*. Nancy portrayed Maddalena—usually sung by a contralto—while the world-renowned tenor Jussi Björling sang "La donna è mobile." As I later discovered, Nancy had also studied and worked with legendary dance figures like Antony Tudor, Martha Graham, and Agnes de Mille.

When the opera season ended that summer, Nancy returned to New York. As she recalls, she was rehearsing *Aida* at the Met when she received a message: "There's a Mr. Kolodin on the phone. He said his wife wants to talk to you." Nancy called my mother, who told her, "We have extra tickets to the opening of the Bolshoi Ballet, and I'd like you to go with my son. Just so you know, he's separated but not divorced." Nancy's reply was immediate. "I'd love to go," she said. "My friends are all gay, or married men on the make."

Nancy and Bill Zeckendorf at their wedding with Bill's "Granny Levy" (left)

Nancy and Bill at the Taj Mahal

I was less enthusiastic. But my mother was insistent. She thought it would be nice for me to go to the ballet with someone who knew something about dance—and she didn't like my girlfriends. So reluctantly I took Nancy to the ballet. Our first meeting wasn't auspicious: we were thrilled with the Bolshoi but not with each other. Nancy was dressed all in black, with her hair pulled back in a bun. I thought she looked like a nun.

But from that unpromising start, our romance took off, and we were married in October 1963 in the Regency Room at the Astor Hotel, which my father owned. I'm grateful my mother persisted; Nancy has been the joy of my life.

After we were married, Nancy retired from dancing but became a star fund-raiser for the arts. In 1965, she began a fifteen-year association with American Ballet Theatre, serving on their board and chairing thirty galas for them. She was also a trustee of the Dance Notation Bureau for more than a decade.

Santa Fe is an unusual city, where nature and the arts are pursued with equal fervor. We are the third-largest art market in the United States, after New York and Los Angeles, but the real cultural heart of the area is the Santa Fe Opera, housed in a semi-open-air theater in the foothills outside town. When we moved to the Southwest, Nancy put her fund-raising prowess to good use on the opera board, serving as its president and chairman. One of her first achievements was organizing the Opera Gala. Held in the Eldorado Hotel ballroom, the gala drew three hundred people its first year. It remains a highlight of the Santa Fe social season, regularly raising some $500,000 for the opera.

Nancy also played a pivotal role in the expansion and renovation of the opera house, working closely with John Crosby, the founder of the Santa Fe Opera. The opera's first home, from its inaugural season in 1957 until it burned down a decade later, was an open-air amphitheater. The building that replaced it had spectacular views, but the audience kept getting rained on through an opening in the roof. By the 1990s, the opera was drawing audiences from around the globe, and John thought a better theater was needed. Nancy spearheaded the drive to raise $21 million—an unheard-of amount for Santa Fe—to totally rebuild the opera house. The new building, designed by James Stewart Polshek, an architect from New York, was finished in time for the 1998 season. An architectural marvel with a soaring suspended roof, the opera house has won numerous design awards. It was renamed the Crosby Theatre after John's death in 2002.

Nancy didn't stop with the opera. She devoted herself to the Lensic, raising $9 million to turn the old movie house into a

Second Santa Fe Opera house, built in 1967 (left)

Opera founder John Crosby with Nancy Zeckendorf

Exterior view of the new Santa Fe Opera house (top)

Interior of the opera house

state-of-the-art performance space and overseeing its transformation. And she continues to be a central force in supporting the arts. Few people have done as much as Nancy to benefit the community. But never in a million years did we expect the honors we've received, especially being named Santa Fe Living Treasures in 2011.

Scenic Views

Los Miradores

Los Miradores is unique in Santa Fe. No other condo project in town has the quality of housing that's there. It is very well run, and the people who bought units have done very well.

EARL POTTER, attorney

My first project in Santa Fe was also one of my first ground-up developments. In the early 1980s, long before we relocated, I built a luxury condominium development in the historic Museum Hill area of Santa Fe, two miles from the Plaza. Nancy named the gated community Los Miradores. *Miradores* means "viewpoints" or "places to look from," and the name couldn't be more fitting. The views from the property are magnificent, which was a major selling point.

The project came to me through Don Elliott, a lawyer on Long Island University's board of trustees, which I was chairing at the time. Don represented St. John's, a liberal arts college in Annapolis, Maryland, that had a satellite campus in Santa Fe.

The college needed cash, and it owned eighteen and a half acres of land next to the New Mexico campus that it wanted to sell. Would I be interested? I didn't have much going in New York just then—the Columbia was still in the planning stage—and this would be a chance to build.

I made an all-cash offer for the tract, with an option on another twenty acres—the valley site—nearby. Then St. John's had second thoughts: the property was part of a 160-acre preserve that had been a gift to the school, and they decided that selling it—even to save the college—would be against the spirit of the gift. So they turned down my offer with a counteroffer: a ninety-nine-year lease on the land. I took the lease—my first mistake.

My original partner in the deal disappeared early on. Someone suggested David Ater: "If you can get him, it will be the *Good Housekeeping* seal of approval for the project." Ater, a highly respected Santa Fe banker and real estate investor, agreed to step in as co-developer. Over the next seven years, as we built out the complex, David oversaw development and was able to keep the project on track despite the many obstacles we encountered.

Los Miradores was one of the first luxury condo complexes in Santa Fe, so it's no surprise we met resistance. The fact that I

Rendering of Los Miradores

Los Miradores condominiums, Santa Fe

was a developer who built skyscrapers in New York raised a red flag in a town where two stories is considered tall. I like to think we developed Los Miradores with sensitivity to the concerns of local residents and respect for our surroundings. But the path was rocky nonetheless.

The college community objected to our presence, and neighbors cried foul every time we felled a tree. We were all over the front page of the *Santa Fe Reporter* with headlines like "New York Developer Comes to Santa Fe and Knocks Down Piñons." Never mind that we had budgeted $250,000 for replanting the area with piñon, juniper, and native grasses. We did our best to head off claims that we were "raping" the land by demonstrating our support for local building traditions.

I had first asked Nancy to be the design consultant on the project, but it became apparent that we needed her talents for overall supervision. Los Miradores marked her debut as a project manager, and she was a natural. Nancy is highly disciplined, organized, and a stickler for detail—essential qualities for coordinating a complicated building project. While I was back in New York building the Columbia, she was flying back and forth to Santa Fe, working closely with the architect, Wayne Lloyd of McHugh-Lloyd Associates, and the interior designer, Fritz Kailer. Equally important was making sure the project conformed to the Santa Fe Historic Design Review Board's exacting standards. Nancy and David Ater bought some acreage across Calle Picacho to the north of Los Miradores, dividing it into six lots and restricting any houses to one story. That allowed us to maximize views from the north-facing condos.

The complex is modeled on a traditional Southwestern village, with low, semidetached adobe houses clustered around courtyards. We planned to build fifty-six units; in the end there were fifty-two, since two of the units were doubles. The first nineteen, which included four model units, were ready for occupancy in July 1983. We built the rest in stages, two and three at a time, as pre-sales came in, delivering the last condo in early 1991.

Interiors of the two- and three-bedroom units are spacious and well laid out, with high ceilings and luxurious appointments. Nancy and David worked with the architects to allow some customization of the units, but any modifications had to stay within the overall design scheme. Amenities for the residents include a swimming pool, a small gym, and a tennis court.

All the elements were in place for Los Miradores to succeed, but there was a major deal breaker that I hadn't factored in. The leasehold arrangement was unacceptable to the well-to-do Texans who were our target buyers. To them, ownership meant land they could leave to their grandchildren, not leased property with a structure on it. I brought in Earl Potter, a local lawyer, who negotiated with St. John's to extend the lease another hundred years, for 199 years in all, with the rent prepaid in full. To get the extension, we had to give up our option on the valley site. The longer lease eased buyers' concerns, but still our sales lagged.

And sluggish sales weren't the only snag. Unbeknownst to us, our architects were also at work on a competing project, the Casas de San Juan, and they stalled Los Miradores to get the other one online first. As if that wasn't enough, our original

Nancy Zeckendorf on Los Miradores construction site (top)

Nancy and Bill Zeckendorf at home at Los Miradores

project manager was also managing construction at Casas de San Juan. We discovered he wasn't keeping a close eye on Los Miradores when Nancy got a call saying that the fireplace in one of the condos had been built into the wrong room. It was at that point that Nancy took over as project manager.

Los Miradores was a small development, and I figured it would take only a couple of years to build. But I was used to building vertically. Once you start a high-rise, you generally don't stop until it's all the way up. In Santa Fe, development is horizontal, and a complex like Los Miradores is built out in phases, adding inventory in response to demand. As Los

Miradores dragged on, we paid off our development loan, but I lost my $3 million equity in the project. The leasehold alone cost $5 million and put us 10 percent over budget.

Though financially disappointing for us, Los Miradores was profitable for the buyers. And it set new standards in design, winning a prestigious PCBC Gold Nugget Award for an "exceptional concept in design, planning, and development" that improved the community. The trees we planted on the property make it one of the prettiest spots in Santa Fe. Nancy and I lived in three different units in Los Miradores before we built the first of our two houses in Sierra del Norte.

Successful Site Planning

Sierra del Norte

Sierra del Norte was the most complicated deal and best piece of work I ever did as a land-use lawyer. Basically we had to negotiate the design of each building site. There was a city councilor who had gone to planning school, and I remember negotiating with her the location of the building pads on every piece of property.

EARL POTTER, attorney

While Los Miradores failed to meet our expectations, Sierra del Norte, a land subdivision we developed, was just the opposite. The deal was complicated, but the project wound up a success in every way.

In 1989, we purchased 365 acres in the foothills on the northeastern side of Santa Fe, just ten minutes from downtown. David Ater brought us into the deal. The property was originally part of a 2,100-acre parcel of undeveloped land that had belonged to a group of investors, but it had been foreclosed. David had been

Entrance to Bill and Nancy Zeckendorf's house at Sierra del Norte, Santa Fe (left)

Living room with view southwest to the Jemez Mountains

retained by Sandia Savings and Loan to figure out something to do with the property. As part of his fee arrangement with the bank, he could buy some or all of the land if he could clear up the legal and approval issues. David deserves great credit for handling the project so ably from beginning to end.

The zoning on the property was complicated. We had a legal right to develop all 365 acres, though in reality, some of the terrain was too rugged to build on. Earl Potter, acting as our attorney, worked out a deal by which we would develop only part of the land, setting aside seventy or so acres as green space. We then carved out 165 development lots. There are now 116 houses in the complex, with only 15 or so empty lots remaining.

We closed on the land in 1989 intending to develop it in four stages. That would have involved submitting requests for approvals at each stage, so Earl and David made a smart move. They worked out a master development plan that allowed us to get all the necessary approvals up front. The green space no doubt smoothed the way.

Another reason the deal was complicated was that we had to negotiate with three different neighborhood associations, as well as the city, to install the infrastructure. Our roads and all our utilities had to be run through the three neighborhoods to connect up to existing systems. Earl also had to get city approval for the plan of each individual building site. We buried the utilities—sewers, water, electric, telephone—underground and placed strict covenants on siting and architecture to make sure the houses blended into the surrounding landscape and didn't block the views.

When we began work on Sierra del Norte, another luxury development, Las Campanas, was also starting up in Santa Fe. That project was offering extensive amenities, including two golf courses and a clubhouse. We chose to take a different route. Rather than amenities, we emphasized the natural beauty of the land, the views, and the proximity to downtown. That was definitely the right tack. Golf isn't a major selling point in Santa Fe; more people come here for the opera, the Chamber Music Festival, and Indian Market, as well as for the art galleries, museums, and restaurants. Our location made all of that immediately accessible.

The biggest problem we faced in developing Sierra del Norte was the financing. Initially we had a development loan from CorEast Savings Bank of Richmond, Virginia. But when we were well along in the development process and had borrowed several million dollars, the savings and loan crisis hit. CorEast was taken over by the Resolution Trust Corporation,

The wine room in the Zeckendorf house (left)

The music room with William Zeckendorf Sr.'s I.M. Pei–designed desk

a government entity formed to resolve S&L failures. Suddenly the RTC owned our property, and in 1991, they forced us to suspend development. My son Will spent days trying to work out a solution; in the end, RTC decided not to foreclose but to give us six months to pay off our loan. Finally, David was able, through his banking connections—he was president of the First National Bank of Santa Fe from 1970 to 1980 and treasurer of the New Mexico Bankers Association—to get the property refinanced by the Albuquerque National Bank. He had to personally guarantee the loan, so we gave him a bigger percentage of equity in Sierra del Norte and made him a full partner.

We resumed work in 1993 and finished the project the following year. With most of the lots sold, we distributed the remaining tracts among the partners as longer-term investments and dissolved the development partnership.

The first house Nancy and I built for ourselves in Sierra del Norte was handsome, but our current one is spectacular. Nancy designed it with her good friend Santa Fe interior designer Greg Teakle. The site is one of the most beautiful in the complex, and the house itself was meticulously conceived down to the last detail. We spend most of our time in a large airy room with a fireplace, an open kitchen, and a dining table in front of broad windows that offer sweeping views of the city and the Jemez Mountains. A temperature-controlled wine room safeguards my extensive collection of Burgundies. And my father's desk, designed for him by I.M. Pei, has pride of place in my music room.

The timing of Sierra del Norte was right, and despite the delays and the expense of installing the utilities underground, it was a financial success. That allowed me to pay down my debts from New York.

Introducing Luxury

The Eldorado Hotel and the Hotel Santa Fe

It would be hard to imagine any other individual or company that has contributed more to the community than has the Eldorado, Santa Fe's largest hotel and its only four-star one.

MALCOLM PYNN, "The Eldorado Hotel Story"

We were in the middle of building Los Miradores in 1983 when Robert Love, a real estate broker from New York who was then living in Santa Fe, came to us and said, "There's a property downtown you should buy, and you need to build a hotel on it. You need a decent place for potential buyers to stay when they come to Santa Fe to look at condominiums in Los Miradores."

He had a point. At the time the only hotels downtown were La Fonda, La Posada—essentially a collection of cottages—and the Inn at Loretto, which wasn't the upscale hotel and spa it is today. The property Robert Love had in mind was a two-acre site with the Big Jo Lumber Company on it.

Nancy Zeckendorf in front of the Big Jo Lumber Company

A Santa Fe institution, Big Jo's had been owned by the same family, the Hillyers, for more than sixty years. They were anxious to sell. The property had already gone to contract once, but the buyer had backed out, which is how Robert Love found out it was up for sale. As soon as we expressed interest, two more buyers showed up. The competition was fierce.

The Hillyers, represented by two Hillyer daughters and their husbands, had named their price. Robert Love started negotiating with them, but he wasn't making any headway. At that point Nancy stepped in. She grew up in a small town in Pennsylvania, where her family owned the town's lumberyard. She realized how important the business was to the Hillyers, and as soon as she sat down and started talking ten-penny nails and two-by-fours, they were charmed.

I asked Earl Potter to take over the negotiations from Robert Love. Having been burned once, the Hillyers wanted nothing more than to find a buyer who wouldn't back out. "Give us some assurance you're going to be able to close this deal," they told Earl. So I wrote a letter to Manufacturers Hanover in New York, and they wrote back saying, "Bill Zeckendorf is one of our most valued clients. We're happy to loan him $15 million to do this transaction."

That's all the Hillyers needed. The property was ours.

But buying the property was just the first of our challenges. Right away we faced community opposition. I'd already had a taste of that with Los Miradores, but here the outcry was even louder. First of all, we were destroying Big Jo's, a beloved local institution. And then we were proposing to build the biggest hotel in Santa Fe and the tallest building downtown. Zoning was going to be an issue: existing regulations limited us to four stories, but we needed five to accommodate the number of guest rooms and amount of public space that would make the project work financially. We would also need the approval of the Historic Design Review Board. Santa Fe has the second-oldest historic preservation design ordinance in the country and by far the most comprehensive. Ultimately, Wayne Lloyd, our architect, was helpful in getting the plans through the board.

But before we could even get to that, we had to decide what to do with Big Jo's. We couldn't just tear it down: it was a much-loved local landmark. Somebody came up with the idea of finding a buyer and relocating the store. We sold the Big Jo name and inventory to the C de Baca family, who reopened the store on Siler Road, where it's still going strong. That was, in a sense, our first historic preservation effort, and it was an important part of the deal. The C de Baca family is old Santa Fe, going all the way back to the Coronado expedition of 1540. The patriarch, Richard C de Baca, a retired New Mexico State Police chief, decided to affiliate with True Value, a hardware cooperative, but the store continues to be very much a family-run operation. It took a while to close the sale, but we were rewarded by the knowledge that the store had gone to an esteemed local family that would carry on the Big Jo's tradition.

Our second problem was getting the design approved by the Historic Design Review Board. Our strategy here rested on my idea of pitching the building as an anchor for the western end of the Plaza, balancing the Cathedral Basilica of St. Francis of Assisi, which holds down the eastern end. We convinced the review board that Santa Fe needed something substantial downtown, and our hotel would be it. In return, they would give us the bigger building we requested. To our surprise, the board agreed—and without the fight we'd anticipated. We were cleared to build five stories.

With that bridge crossed, we immediately faced another. There was a Spanish Baptist church a hundred or so feet behind our lot, where the Georgia O'Keeffe Museum now stands. Local laws prohibited serving liquor within three hundred feet of a church, which meant we wouldn't be able to get a liquor license. But we couldn't have a hotel without a bar. Now what?

Robert Love came up with another good plan. "Let's move the church," he said. He talked to members of the congregation; it turned out they would be happy to move. It had gotten too crowded downtown, they said, and there wasn't enough parking for their parishioners. Robert found a property on Cerrillos Road,

The Eldorado Hotel, Santa Fe

and we got Stan Davis, our contractor on Los Miradores, to draw up a set of plans for a new church. Robert showed the plans to the church members and said, "Here—you can build this on this piece of property. There'll be enough money from your property downtown to build the new church." We bought the church, then turned around and sold the site to pay for the new church, which was ready at about the same time as the hotel. (Since then, the Spanish Baptist church has closed, but the building is enjoying a new, secular life as the Center for Progress and Justice and the headquarters of the Democratic Party of Santa Fe County.)

While we were designing the hotel, another problem cropped up: we didn't have quite enough land to build the 218 guest rooms we needed. There was a twenty-five-foot strip next to our site, but it was owned by the county courthouse. Fortunately, Earl had been the county attorney and knew the right people to approach. He negotiated a swap whereby the county would sell us the property in exchange for ten parking spaces in the hotel's underground garage. We were reluctant to give up the parking spaces and proposed buying them spaces in another garage instead. But the county land-use administrator didn't trust the structural integrity of the other garage and told Earl, "That thing's going to fall down. I want some good parking spaces down below." They got their spaces in our garage.

We also had to deal with a small house on the property. It dated back to the 1830s, and the Historic Design Review Board wouldn't let us tear it down. Despite investing $250,000 and a lot of effort propping it up, as soon as we started construction on the hotel, the house fell down. We were able to preserve it in name at least: the Old House Restaurant in the Eldorado has been a popular gathering place ever since.

Inevitably if a project is going to make a big impact on a community, somebody is bound to oppose it. A week before we closed, a lawyer—a shady character whose office was near our site—sent us a letter saying he was going to sue to stop the closing because we were interfering with his solar rights. (New Mexico had recently passed a law protecting access to the sun for anyone wanting to install solar panels on their roof.) As it happened, Earl had an associate who had helped write the solar law. So the associate drafted a twenty-page document analyzing the path of the sun and sent it to the lawyer, saying, "Here's why you don't have a claim, and if you sue us, it's going to be a malicious prosecution." That—and a small settlement—shut the lawyer up, and our closing went ahead.

The sun wasn't the only thing we were accused of blocking. Views are a big deal in Santa Fe, and there were complaints that the hotel would limit the view of the mountains. But the economy was in a slump at the time, and the business community wanted our hotel to succeed. At the closing, the man who owned the title company turned to Earl and said, "The Eldorado is going to be the foundation for the economic success of this town in the next ten years." And he was right.

To finance construction, I looked for a hotel company to invest in the Eldorado and then run it. Frank Palmer, who was working

The Hotel Santa Fe, Santa Fe

for Aircoa, a Denver-based hotel management firm, came in as a partner and also suggested bringing in the Guardian Life Insurance Company from New York. Construction proceeded relatively smoothly, and we finished on time at a total cost of about $26 million. In all, from closing on the property to opening for business, the Eldorado took about three years to build.

The grand opening in December 1985 was quite an affair. Several rooms hadn't been completed and the plumbing was still somewhat unreliable, but the town flocked to see what we had done.

We still hear the odd complaint about the Eldorado's size, but most of the grousing stopped once it was clear that the hotel filled an important niche in town and was indeed an economic driver. Before we built the Eldorado, Santa Fe had no banquet rooms or meeting spaces of any size, so the hotel played a major role in developing the city's convention business. Its location and pampering ways also made the Eldorado a favorite place to stay for music lovers coming to town for the opera and the Chamber Music Festival. Then, too, the Eldorado earned praise for hosting local groups. The annual gala that Nancy launched to raise money for the opera was for many years held at the hotel.

For all that, the Eldorado wasn't an instant success. But by its third year it took off, and occupancy has been about 80 percent ever since. Initially we were drawing out $300,000 a year for our share of the hotel. Later, as tourism in Santa Fe fell off, we sold our interest in the Eldorado at a loss.

From 1986 to 1994, we had an outstanding manager, Paul Margetson, overseeing the Eldorado. A British hotelier who had previously managed world-class hotels in Europe, Asia, and the Caribbean, Margetson was so good that I agreed to develop another hotel, the Hotel Santa Fe, largely to keep him in town.

The 134-room hotel was a partnership with the Picuris, a Native American tribe. In 1988, while I was developing the Crowne Plaza Hotel in New York, I got a letter from the parent company, the Holiday Corporation, saying that they had looked at a piece of property in Santa Fe that would be ideal for a Holiday Inn. Would I like to develop it with them?

I told Earl Potter I didn't want to develop the property on my own and asked if he knew anyone locally who might want to explore the possibility with me. Earl's wife, Deborah, suggested we contact another of his clients, Joe Schepps. Earl arranged a lunch for us to meet. Afterward, the three of us went and stood at the corner of Cerrillos Road and Paseo de Peralta and looked at the property. The land was owned by the Yates family of Yates Petroleum, but at that point it was a trailer park. Richard Yates,

Patio of the Hotel Santa Fe

the family member who was living in Santa Fe, was an architect, which made the deal particularly difficult. The Yates family wouldn't sell the property unless we hired Richard to design the hotel. He didn't have the experience to do it by himself, but once we worked out a deal, Richard collaborated with Jerry Exline, an accomplished hotel architect. The two men came up with an innovative X-shaped design that preserved numerous century-old trees, making the hotel seem instantly at home in its surroundings.

Holiday Corporation had been denied permission to build, though, so Joe and I formed a partnership to develop the hotel. Paul Margetson came in as our operating partner. Earl was our lawyer on the deal, and he and Deborah joined us as partners.

By this time, the savings and loan crisis had hit the Southwest with full force, so we had a huge problem finding financing. Eventually we were introduced to a man from Albuquerque who told us about the Indian Financing Act, passed in 1974 as a way to attract outside investment in tribal ventures. If Native Americans made up 51 percent of a partnership, it was possible to get government financing for a project. The Bureau of Indian Affairs suggested we partner with the Picuris—the name means "those who paint"—a tribe whose pueblo is sixty miles north of Santa Fe, in Taos County.

It took us about three years to put the deal together. It was tough going from the start and often looked as if it would fall apart. We discovered that the man from Albuquerque had misrepresented the government financing, and that the $10 million we wanted for construction would be a third of all the money available under this program for the entire country that year. Still, we made it happen. We went to the Bureau of Indian Affairs in Washington and managed to get the money.

In a 2008 article in *Indian Country News,* the head of the Picuris called the Hotel Santa Fe "a source of pride" for the tribe. It had given them not only income but also "a new life and a new outlook." It was the first off-reservation hotel joint venture between a Native American tribe and a nontribal group.

We opened the Hotel Santa Fe in 1993, and it was a success. The Eldorado didn't like the idea of Paul splitting his time between the two hotels, however, so he left the Eldorado to devote himself full time to the Hotel Santa Fe. I sold my interest in the hotel, but Paul is still a part owner with Earl and Deborah.

Restoring a Landmark

The Lensic Performing Arts Center

The Lensic is a gift to Santa Fe that would not have happened without the combined energy of Bill and Nancy. The project confirmed Bill's leadership and vision. And Nancy's dedication to the renovation, from fund-raising to daily on-site project management, was amazing.

DAVID ATER, development partner

Our last project in Santa Fe—and the one Nancy and I are proudest of—is the Lensic Performing Arts Center. I negotiated a long-term lease on a historic theater building, found an architect for the restoration, and put together a group of people to help us with loans and city approvals. From there, Nancy was the driving force behind the project and remains the chairman of the board and a trusted advisor today.

The Lensic is a 1930s-era theater with an interesting history. The original developer was a Syrian immigrant named Nathan Salmon, who began as a cart peddler, then opened a dry goods store in Santa Fe. He bought up property until, at his death in 1941, he was one of the richest men in New Mexico. Along the way he became a theater operator of note, and with his son-in-law, E. John Greer, he created the Lensic, a Spanish-style theater and dance hall. It was his gift to the people of Santa Fe, Salmon said, out of gratitude for his success. Soon the Lensic was the center of the town's social and cultural life, with live vaudeville shows, films, classical music, and dance. It later evolved into a movie house that hosted film premieres with stars like Rita Hayworth, Judy Garland, and Ronald Reagan. By the time we moved to Santa Fe, the Lensic was an ordinary movie house, managed by United Artists, and had seen better days.

In 1998 Nancy told me that a local chamber music group that had been using the theater for their concerts had just found out it was no longer available to them. People had been saying that Santa Fe needed a performing arts center for all the local groups to use. So before Nancy could finish, I was on the phone to the Greers, the Lensic's owners. But they said they could do nothing. It was up to United Artists, who held the lease to the theater.

Painting of the Lensic by Odon Hullenkremer

Then I had an idea: United Artists was in a slump. Maybe they would sell us their lease, and then we could turn the Lensic into the nonprofit theater we had envisioned. I called our friend Richard Brandt to see if he would help. I knew Richard from the College of Santa Fe, where we were both trustees. At the time, he was chairman of Trans-Lux, a communications company that owned a chain of movie theaters. With Richard's help, I approached United Artists about buying the lease. It took six months of negotiations, but finally UA told us, "Sure, you can buy the lease—for $450,000."

Buying the United Artists lease was key to going forward with the project. But we would still need to upgrade the theater. If we were going to sink a lot of money into renovations, we should own, not lease, the property. I approached the Greers about buying the Lensic. They refused to sell, so I asked them for a seventy-five-year lease. More than a year of negotiations followed.

The Lensic was viewed with great nostalgia by longtime residents of Santa Fe—and presumably by the Greer family as well. The theater was named for Nathan Salmon's six grandchildren: Lensic spelled out the initials of their first names. The family insisted that anyone who took over the theater keep the name. Even after we agreed to that, negotiations dragged on. Alexis Greer, the family member in charge of their real estate, was in favor of granting us the lease, but one of her cousins flatly opposed it. Finally, the family patriarch agreed to intervene. We got our lease at last.

Now we had an even bigger problem: money for renovations. Though the Lensic still had a certain stately charm, inside it was a wreck. It would require a complete overhaul to turn it into a modern facility that could function as a legitimate theater, dance space, symphony hall, lecture stage, and auditorium for everything from chamber music to rock concerts to charity events. Among the challenges: poor acoustics, no backstage to speak of, no loft space to fly scenery, no dressing rooms for performers, no green room for guests.

I said to Nancy, "I put together the deal. Now you have to raise the money." Her reply was, "I don't want to." She had just stepped down from the opera board and was looking forward to a much-needed rest. But there's no bigger champion of the arts than Nancy. So she set to work, raising $9 million to restore the Lensic to its former glory and transform it into a state-of-the-art facility capable of hosting every kind of performance. It was a massive undertaking, but Nancy was determined. Once we started construction, it was completed in a year.

As usual, there were complications. The Lensic straddles three different building zones, with three different sets of regulations, and it's located in the heart of the Santa Fe Historic District. But for once we faced no opposition. The entire town was in favor of the Lensic's revival. People who grew up in Santa Fe have fond memories of it as the place where they went on their first date and stole their first kiss in the balcony. And though by the early 1990s there was a lot of good music in Santa Fe, there was no good theater to present it in. So everyone rallied behind bringing the Lensic back to life.

It wasn't easy, however. We had to preserve the classic Spanish-style facade and restore the interior ornamentation while completely gutting and rebuilding the backstage area. We hired Klinger Constructors, an Albuquerque company with expertise in both theater construction and historic renovation. They punched a hole in the back wall and added forty feet to the stage, then created fly space overhead and space below the stage for trap doors, dressing rooms, and storage. The orchestra pit was enlarged and fitted with a lift to raise and lower the platform depending on the size of the orchestra.

Then there was the matter of upgrading the acoustics. We hired sound engineer Jack Purcell, who had been the acoustician for all three Santa Fe Opera houses. As we were considering various approaches, Marc Neikrug, artistic director of the Santa Fe Chamber Music Festival, and the violinist and conductor Pinchas Zukerman, who performed with Marc almost every summer, became interested in the project. Marc later helped

The Lensic during renovation

Nancy get funding for both the sound system and the orchestra shell. Pinchas, meanwhile, convinced us to go to Ottawa and listen to the sound system in the National Arts Centre, where he was director of the orchestra. Jack flew to Ottawa and the next morning called me and said, "You have to do this at the Lensic. It will work perfectly for what you want." The sound system cost $350,000, but Jack was right: it was perfect. It allows us to reset the auditorium electronically according to the sound requirements of any type of performance.

Artisans from Conrad Schmitt Studios, a restoration firm, scraped years of grime off the plasterwork, repaired it, and then stenciled, gilded, and touched up the decorative cartouches and other gewgaws throughout the interior. They repainted the decorative arches uncovered in the renovation and restored the original lobby murals depicting scenes of the Southwest.

The renovated auditorium required new seating. We couldn't find what we wanted anywhere in the United States in the quantity we needed at a price within our budget. I went online and tracked down a company in South America that manufactured theater seats and could fill an order for 830. When opening night was fast approaching and the seats hadn't arrived, I said to Nancy, "Well, then I'll call them." She said something like, "Don't be silly. You don't even speak Spanish." That didn't stop me. I picked up the phone, dialed the company in Colombia, and said to the man who answered, "I'm Bill Zeckendorf from Santa Fe." And he said, "Hi, this is Juan." The seats were on their way, he told me. Frank Ortiz Jr., a former U.S. ambassador to Guatemala, Argentina, and other countries who lived in Santa Fe, helped us get the shipment through customs and on a truck to the Lensic. Then Juan and his workers flew up from Colombia and installed the seats in two days—just in time for our opening in April 2001.

Nancy not only supervised the renovations but also hired a general manager. She had a lucky find in Robert Martin: as executive and artistic director he has been responsible for making the Lensic into a truly outstanding performing arts center. As chairman of the board, Nancy is a ready advisor and the chief fund-raiser.

Restored to its former glory but updated for a new century, the Lensic Performing Arts Center is today one of Santa Fe's most popular attractions, with a packed, year-round schedule of events. True to its nonprofit mission, the theater hosts Pro Musica, the Santa Fe Symphony, the Santa Fe Chamber Music Festival, the Santa Fe Concert Association (now Performance Santa Fe), the Aspen Santa Fe Ballet, the Lannan Foundation's lecture series, and other local organizations.

I serve on the Lensic board and do what I can to be useful. When the Metropolitan Opera announced its Live in HD

Exterior view of the restored Lensic, Santa Fe (left)

Lensic stage

program, I suggested we simulcast the programs at the Lensic. Nancy thought that would be impossible, because the Met had long since made arrangements with the participating theaters. But I picked up the phone and called the general director of the Santa Fe Opera, and with a lot of back and forth—along with help from the president of the opera board and her husband, who was president of the Met Opera board, as well as a Lensic board member who was also on the Santa Fe Opera board—we got the Met's approval to screen the broadcasts at the Lensic.

I learned a long time ago not to assume that anything is impossible.

My Passions

People may not think of me as a passionate man, but when I believe in something, I commit to it fully. You could say it's pretty obvious I'm passionate about development and the built environment. What many people may not know, however, are the things I'm committed to in my private life.

For years I was passionate about horseback riding, spending weekends on the trails in Westchester County. Unfortunately, my riding days ended after repeated back surgeries to repair the damage from a very bad fall, not to mention all those hours in the saddle.

My longstanding love of classical music, on the other hand, continues to grow—as does my collection of recordings. Since moving to Santa Fe I've had the good fortune to serve on the board of the Santa Fe Chamber Music Festival.

And then there's wine, an enthusiasm of my father's that became one of mine. I collect fine wines and, like most wine lovers, enjoy sharing my favorites. Few things are more gratifying than introducing the young or uninitiated to an outstanding vintage.

There are certain other activities that out of love or honor I've pursued with dedication, if not outright zeal. One is community service. Following in my father's footsteps, I served on the board of trustees of Long Island University for thirty-six years.

Last, but far from least, is my family. Nancy is the love of my life. And I'm immensely proud of my sons and my grandchildren. They're not only carrying on the Zeckendorf name but the passion for real estate development and fine architecture.

An Inherited Taste

The first time I met Bill was when my husband, Frank Williams, and I were invited to Bill and Nancy's for dinner. I'm from Chile, so I arrived with a $2.98 bottle of Chilean wine. I was mortified to find out Bill was in Tastevin; Frank had forgotten to tell me. But when I handed Bill the wine, he took it and very carefully examined the label and asked about the winery. He was so interested. Here it was, this $2.98 bottle of wine, but he gave it his full attention.

VERONICA GARAYCOCHEA-WILLIAMS

After Nancy, my greatest passion is wine. Burgundies in particular, though I've been known to pull a cork on a fine Bordeaux now and then.

An appreciation of wine is without question something I inherited from my father. Like everything else he did, he went into wine collecting in a big way. On a trip to France in the 1950s, he met a vintner and decided to buy some of his wine.

Bill Zeckendorf's induction into Tastevin, 1958, by Grand Officier H. Gregory Thomas, far left, and Grand Sénéchal Clifford T. Weihman, second from left

Dad didn't buy just a few bottles, however; he bought three or four hundred cases—all Burgundy. He had enjoyed wine before then, but after that trip he began collecting seriously. At his estate in Connecticut, my father had an exceptional wine cellar designed by I.M. Pei. It was an open cellar: I could take anything I wanted. I'd always had a taste for wine, but my father's cellar was something special. Of particular note were his 1945 Burgundies, as well as some '47s, '53s, and '55s. In all, he had about 24,000 bottles, which I inherited.

I, too, have been collecting wine for years. I kept a wine cellar at our house in Chappaqua, New York, and when Nancy and I built our present house in Santa Fe, we made sure to include a temperature-controlled wine room. My collection of Burgundies includes my particular favorites, the Musignys. My pride and joy was a 1934 Musigny Comte Georges de Vogüé from my father's cellar.

My father was an early member of La Confrérie des Chevaliers du Tastevin, a society of Burgundy connoisseurs. (Tastevin—pronounced "tat-vin"—comes from the *tâtevin,* the traditional wine tasting cup used by winemakers and connoisseurs.) Founded in France in 1934, Tastevin launched an American branch in 1939. When I joined the New York Sous-Commanderie, or chapter, in 1958, I was by far the youngest member. From 1991 to 2000 I served as Grand Sénéchal, or president, of the New York chapter. My son Will, who shares my appreciation of wine, joined Tastevin in 1990 and is now Grand Sénéchal.

Bill Zeckendorf with his son Will at a Tastevin event

Tastevin is a convivial organization, centered on Burgundy-infused dinners and trips to some of the great wineries of the Burgundy region. In France, the banquets are rollicking affairs, with the Cadets de Bourgogne—a chorus of vineyard workers—singing traditional drinking songs with lyrics like *"Si je meurs, je veux qu'on m'enterre / dans une cave òu il y a du bon vin.* (If I die, I want to be buried / in a cellar full of good wine.)"

In 1986 the Santa Fe chapter hosted the Grand Conseil de la Commanderie—the Tastevin board of directors—at a dinner in the Eldorado. That night, the Old House Restaurant was a sea of red-and-gold robes—our traditional ceremonial dress—with a mariachi band playing in the background. Quite a blend of cultures.

Tastevin isn't just a giant party, however. We're serious about wine, and about fostering greater appreciation of Burgundy's wine producers and fine wines. The Commanderie d'Amérique set up a nonprofit foundation in 1979. In 2000, Kelly Shannon, a former Grand Pilier Général d'Amérique, asked me to head up the foundation. Its purpose is to raise awareness of the wines and culture of Burgundy, but when I took over, it had been inactive for years. I thought a good use of the foundation's reputation and resources would be to educate future winegrowers. I approached the director of viticulture and enology at the University of California, Davis, about creating a laureate program for its graduates to study with top wine producers in Burgundy. Since 2002, two fellows every year have spent four or so months learning all aspects of winemaking from their Burgundian hosts. The program is mutually beneficial. The growers say they pick up new techniques from their interns,

Bill Zeckendorf receiving the Tastevin d'Or, for outstanding service, from Kelly Shannon

and the laureates have gone on to work for top American winemakers in California, Oregon, and New York.

To help raise funds for the foundation, I produced a DVD on Burgundy that includes a brief history of Tastevin and the laureate program. It also features interviews with French Tastevin officers by the wine expert Hugh Johnson, along with a segment from Johnson's thirteen-part WGBH series on wine.

Giving Back

For a while, Bill Jr. didn't say much at LIU board meetings. But after his father died, he blossomed. Bill was a steady and reliable supporter of the university. He did everything right.

MARY M. LAI, Long Island University treasurer emerita and former CFO

Philanthropy runs deep in my family. My father instilled in me a strong sense of helping others. My years in Santa Fe have provided an opportunity to support several organizations whose good works I respect. But long before I came to Santa Fe, I was involved in worthy causes in New York.

I was a director of the Boy Scouts of America Greater New York Councils, and am the proud recipient of their Silver Beaver Award, which recognizes distinguished service to the scouting program. Professionally, I served as a director of the Realty Foundation of New York and as governor of the Real Estate Board of New York.

My longest-running commitment was to Long Island University, now one of the largest private universities in America. Starting with my father, three generations of Zeckendorfs have served on the LIU board of trustees.

LIU was founded in Brooklyn, New York, in the 1920s as a nonsectarian school with an open-door policy. Its mission—Access and Excellence—expresses the university's aim to provide a superior education to people from all walks of life. Mary Lai, who was CFO of LIU from 1947 through 2003, likes to say, "We may not be as prestigious as Duke or Princeton, but we made a bigger difference in our students' lives." LIU served the waves of immigrants coming to the United States in the 1930s and 1940s, and remained committed to diversity through the years when many private colleges implemented strict quotas for Jews and other minorities.

My father joined the LIU board in 1942, when the College of Podiatry, whose board he was serving on, merged with the university. At the time, LIU was, as Dad put it, "a diminutive and unaccredited school temporarily settled in a loft building in Brooklyn." After enrollment dropped precipitously during World War II, LIU was forced into bankruptcy. When it came out of receivership in 1947, my father was named chairman of the board. One of the other board members was John McGrath; years later, when McGrath was chairman of the East New York Savings Bank, he financed my first hotel, the Mayfair House.

Bill Zeckendorf, David Steinberg, and Derek Bok, president of Harvard University, at Steinberg's inauguration as president of LIU, Brooklyn, 1985

During the late 1940s, my father was involved in a Title I slum clearance project in Brooklyn with Robert Moses, New York's "master planner," who was intent on turning downtown Brooklyn into a civic center. Dad gave LIU $500,000 to buy seven and a half acres in the downtown area to establish its first campus. The old Paramount Theater, which was on the site, was converted into a gym, classrooms, cafeteria, and offices.

My father remained a trustee of LIU until his death in 1976. I joined the board in 1958, serving as chairman from 1984 until 1992. I resigned in 1994, after I moved to Santa Fe. From 2000 to 2009, my son Will was a trustee.

One of the smartest moves I made during my tenure as board chair was hiring David Steinberg as president in 1985. David was a strong academician who improved the quality of scholarship at LIU, as well as an effective administrator. He was also very shrewd. The trustees viewed David's appointment as an opportunity to generate positive press for LIU, and I hired PR honcho Howard Rubenstein to help. Howard suggested we make a splash with a big celebration of David's inauguration at Lincoln Center or Carnegie Hall. But David understood that an event in Manhattan to promote a Long Island– and Brooklyn-based institution was sure to alienate the LIU community. So instead we held a parade in downtown Brooklyn. David told me he still cherishes a photo of the two of us smiling and holding balloons as we marched down Flatbush Avenue alongside Derek Bok, a friend of David's who was then president of Harvard.

Never mind that my father and I were college dropouts: LIU awarded us both honorary degrees. But Dad would be especially proud of another honor conferred by the university: the William Zeckendorf Health Sciences Center, named for us both in recognition of our service to LIU. Designed by Mitchell/Giurgola Architects and dedicated in 1995, the $23 million facility was the first new building on the Brooklyn campus in twenty years.

After I moved to the Southwest, my experience on the LIU board stood me in good stead as a trustee of the College of Santa Fe. Just as my father had helped LIU rebound from

William Zeckendorf Health Sciences Center, LIU, Brooklyn

bankruptcy in the 1940s, I helped guide the College of Santa Fe through a major transition. When enrollment fell a few years ago, we made the difficult decision to close down the college. It reopened the following year under different auspices, as the Santa Fe University of Art and Design. I think it should have been named the "School of Arts in the City of the Arts," but by any name it's thriving.

One of my most gratifying philanthropic efforts since moving to Santa Fe was a joint project with Nancy: establishing the Lensic Performing Arts Center. I was able to draw on my experience as a developer to acquire the building, while Nancy raised the funds and managed the renovation. I continue to be involved as a member of the Lensic board, which Nancy chairs.

Music is a lifelong passion of mine, and it's been a particular pleasure to serve on the executive committee of the Santa Fe Chamber Music Festival. Held over six weeks in July and August, the festival is a highlight of the summer season.

Given all my health problems, I've had a lot of experience—too much—as a patient. At least it served me well as a board member of St. Vincent Hospital in Santa Fe. I helped steer the hospital through a merger with Christus Health, a Catholic hospital, in 2008, then stepped down from the board of Christus St. Vincent in 2012.

Three Generations

As we look around the city every day, we will forever be reminded of what our father accomplished.

ARTHUR ZECKENDORF

For years I was known as the man in the middle—the quiet one between my flamboyant father and my superstar sons, William Lie and Arthur. Now a fourth generation of Zeckendorfs is coming along, and it will be interesting to see where they will fit in. Will they carry on the family business, the Zeckendorf tradition? My granddaughter, Jennifer, is due to graduate from the Columbia Graduate School of Architecture, Planning and Preservation in 2016. My grandson, Arthur III, who has worked for his father and for a real estate investment company, is in the class of 2015 at Columbia Business School.

While I was growing up, my father was the biggest name in real estate development. By the time my sons came along, he was just Grandpère—a colorful character, though they weren't

Will and Arthur Zeckendorf on a trip to St. Bart's

entirely sure why he was famous or what he had achieved. I'm glad they had a chance to spend time with him nonetheless. He adored the boys, and they remember him with great fondness. It was hard not to be captivated by my father's ebullient personality.

Among my favorite memories of early days with my sons are the trips we took to St. Bart's at Christmastime. The island hadn't yet caught on with the international set, so the beaches were uncrowded and the atmosphere relaxed. Those were wonderful, easygoing times, swimming in the Caribbean and relaxing in the sun.

After Will and Arthur went away to prep school and college, I saw much less of them. But they graduated just about the time my career was taking off and I was starting to develop my own projects from the ground up. Both came to work for me. Will started in 1980, after graduation from Tufts, then took time out to attend Harvard Business School before rejoining my team. Arthur started after he graduated from Tufts in 1981, just as we were about to break ground on the Columbia. From then until 1992, when they went out on their own, nearly every one of my projects had at least one of my sons on the job, very often both.

I was a tough boss at times. I expected a lot of everyone who worked for me, and the hours were long. But Will and

Bill Zeckendorf with Will, at left, and Arthur

Arthur were fast learners and hard workers with original ideas, and their contributions to my projects were invaluable.

Away from the job, we saw less of one another. The boys had busy lives, so our time together centered on shared interests and occasional family get-togethers. Will and I share a love of fine wine and are longtime members of Tastevin. Arthur and I share a love of great architecture.

Arthur's two children, Jennie and Artie, now join in conversations about development and real estate. When Jennie visited us in Santa Fe a few years ago, she brought along a project she was working on. What a pleasure it was to pore over the plans together, examining every detail. I was reminded of the collaborative exchanges I had with Frank Williams, Lew Davis, and Jim Freed—and of listening in as my father talked architecture with I.M. Pei.

Will likes to say that the Zeckendorfs are a "dynasty of self-made entrepreneurs." I'm not sure I agree entirely with that assessment, but I understand what he means. I wouldn't have had the career I had without the Zeckendorf name and the lessons passed on by my father. But just as I had to start over from scratch and rebuild after my father's business collapsed, so did Will and Arthur when they went out on their own in 1992. By then I had no portfolio of properties to pass along and was unable to provide them with financial backing. But they've done more than all right.

The third generation of Zeckendorfs is developing in a real estate climate that has changed dramatically since the days when my father and I were active. My sons have followed a different path from my father's or mine. While Dad and I built for buyers at all income levels, Will and Arthur are focusing on the very top of the market, with luxury residential condominiums designed by world-class architects like Robert A. M. Stern and Norman Foster. And while my father and I usually had half a dozen or more projects under way simultaneously, my sons concentrate on one or two buildings at a time.

I couldn't be prouder of my sons. They have an unerring sense of what's right for the times. I'd like to think that's in the Zeckendorf genes. The last project we worked on together, 515 Park Avenue, was the most successful new residential building in New York when the apartments went on sale in 2000. A decade later, my sons' condominium at 15 Central Park West again broke all sales records, and the prices—already in the stratosphere—continue to climb. Their next condominiums—18 Gramercy Park, 50 United Nations Plaza, and 520 Park—are

15 Central Park West, New York (left)

Will and Arthur Zeckendorf at 50 United Nations Plaza construction site, 2014

on track to be just as successful. Not only are the prices setting records but the designs are setting the standard for luxury apartment houses in Manhattan.

In addition to their development activities, Will and Arthur are co-owners of two of New York's most respected real estate firms, Brown Harris Stevens and Halstead Property. With their sharp focus, innate caution, and canny business sense, Will and Arthur are unlikely to fall into the financial traps their father and grandfather couldn't avoid, even if the real estate market takes a downturn.

Thanks to the third generation, the Zeckendorf flag still flies high. I can't wait to see what the fourth generation brings.

Three generations: Bill Zeckendorf with his father and his son Will (left)

Bill Zeckendorf with grandson Arthur III

Granddaughter Jennifer

Summing Up

If I had to sum up my mission as a developer, it might be something like "reclaiming undervalued properties and revitalizing urban centers." There's probably a more poetic way of phrasing it. But my hope is that I've made life better for people in the process.

What interested me most about development was putting the project together—the plan, the financing, the leasing and/or sales, and the design. Did I take enough interest in construction? Probably not. I counted on other people to build the buildings.

It's hard to say what influenced my career the most, but I'd probably cite two things: Worldwide Plaza, the massive project that opened up Eighth Avenue to development, and my father's bankruptcy. After suffering with my father through the demise of his company and personal bankruptcy, I was determined to never let that happen to me. Still, many years later I, too, succumbed to what ultimately took him down. I call it developer's disease.

Developer's disease is a rare but highly contagious condition that afflicts certain developers. They hire the best archi-

Bill Zeckendorf at a 1998 ceremony for the Lehman College Leadership Award with, from left, Arthur, Will, Nancy, Eileen Pei, Frank Williams, and I.M. Pei

tects. Their projects are the most admired. They're financially very successful. They start with one project at a time. Then one project grows into another and another until they have many projects—some would say too many—under way. They begin to take on the most difficult projects, not just putting up buildings but remaking whole neighborhoods. Their goal is no longer making money; it's being a savior. And they are treated royally for their pains. Based on their sterling records, financial institutions rush to provide money, and investors clamor to partner on their projects. And then, just as these developers are riding high, invincible, a deal goes sour or the market turns, and their luck runs out. Developer's disease mows them down.

That's pretty much what happened to me. After a cautious start in the 1970s, by the middle of the 1980s I was the busiest developer in New York City, with a full plate of deals in progress and a full-blown, if undiagnosed, case of developer's disease. I can't blame what happened next entirely on the market collapse at the end of the decade. Nor can I pin it on my Japanese investors, who were pinched by their own economic downturn and unable to help when creditors called my loans. Nor can I lay it at the feet of my American partners, some of whom proved disloyal in a crunch. I can't even put the responsibility on my growing health problems, though constant pain is always an unwelcome distraction. Were I to do my career over, I might undertake fewer projects, juggle fewer balls, and steer clear of personal guarantees. But I wouldn't for a second choose another field.

I can't think of anything more challenging, more satisfying, more frustrating, and more fun than real estate development. It's too bad I didn't leave the game with a bulging portfolio and a hefty bottom line like some of my colleagues. But I have wonderful memories of the heady days in New York and a rewarding second career here in Santa Fe. I can still take pride in my record, in the more than thirty major projects I completed. Like my father and our Zeckendorf relatives before us, I've been a pioneer.

Writing this book was a departure for me. I'm usually a man of few words. When people ask me what I accomplished in my career, I tell them: "Look around New York. The buildings are there."

EPILOGUE

Bill Zeckendorf died on February 12, 2014, just as he was putting the finishing touches on this memoir. At memorials in New York City and Santa Fe, Nancy Zeckendorf remembered him with these words:

You've heard a lot about Bill's achievements in New York, and that's what most people will remember him for. But for the last fifteen years of his life, Bill had a wonderful life and a rewarding second career in New Mexico—different, but just as gratifying.

Bill had never really considered living anywhere but New York until he found himself in Santa Fe. He knew how much I loved New Mexico, and he used to say, "If anything happens to me, you'll just move to Santa Fe." Well, we moved to Santa Fe and guess what? Bill loved it and was very happy.

When we came out that first summer, Bill was very weak from several back operations and was in constant pain. But he never complained, never lost his temper or became cranky. Everyone who knew Bill uses the same expression to describe him: he was a true gentle man.

This gentle man had a middle name. It was Persistence with a capital P—sometimes two capital Ps. Whatever happened, he never gave up.

Bill loved music. His humongous speakers and subwoofer went with us everywhere. He had a great collection of classical music and loved to compare artists and recordings. He had twelve different versions of Beethoven's symphonies, for example, including two by the same conductor recorded at different times. It seemed logical that Bill would be asked to join the Santa Fe Chamber Music Festival board.

Shortly thereafter, he was asked to join the board of the College of Santa Fe, which he saw through the process of becoming the Santa Fe University of Art and Design. Bill was very proud of that.

Then Bill joined the board of St. Vincent Hospital as it merged with Christus Health. He knew a lot about that hospital. He'd spent a lot of time there in recent years.

You've heard about Bill's passion for wine, especially Burgundy. Imagine his joy in discovering that Santa Fe had a chapter of his beloved Tastevin. And then his friend Kelly Shannon asked him to head up the Tastevin Foundation, which had been doing nothing for years. Bill created a scholarship he called the Laureate Program, which every year sends two students from the University of California, Davis, wine program to Burgundy to study French winemaking and experience French culture. He even made a film to promote the program.

A few years after we moved to Santa Fe, Bill had the opportunity to put together another deal. Not a New York deal with a complicated assemblage and a neighborhood-changing high-rise but a deal that would affect the lives of many in Santa Fe. One day I told Bill I'd heard that a local group, Pro Musica, was no longer able to rent the Lensic movie theater for its concerts and that some people felt it was time to create a venue for all the performing arts groups in Santa Fe. I hadn't finished my sentence before Bill was on the phone to the family who owned the theater. No one had been successful in creating a performing arts center before, but persistence will out. Bill put together a group of people who knew how to get things through the city, the banks, and the Historical Styles board. Then he turned to me and said, "You have to raise the money."

After fifteen years of fund-raising for the Santa Fe Opera, I thought I was on a permanent sabbatical, but Bill said, "You have to do it because no one else can." And so we created the Lensic Performing Arts Center in downtown Santa Fe. Now we can't walk down the street without someone coming up to say how much the theater means to them.

Bill went on the Internet and found seats for the theater in Colombia, South America. He was able to get the seats through customs just in time for the opening. Then he read in the *New York Times* that performances of the Metropolitan Opera were being simulcast at movie theaters. "We need to have that at the Lensic," he said. I told him, "I don't think that's possible. They have a contract with Regal Cinemas." Not to be deterred, Bill called the director of the Santa Fe Opera to ask him to cosponsor the simulcasts. And after keeping at it, Bill succeeded. We got permission to screen not only the Met simulcasts but also those of the National Theatre of London.

Bill was quick to say that the memoir he was writing was not about him but about his buildings. He decided to write it so his grandchildren would know what he'd done. The last thing out of his computer before he died was the chapter entitled "Three Generations."

Bill never gave up. A week before his death, he was working on a new idea for promoting the Tastevin scholarship program. When he went off to the hospital for the last time, he was sedated and not very responsive. The attendants put him in the ambulance and headed down the driveway. Then the ambulance stopped, and the driver ran back to the house and said, "He wants his iPhone."

That was Bill.

Nancy Zeckendorf

AFTERWORD

During the early part of my real estate career, I had the privilege of working with my father, William Zeckendorf Jr., on numerous ventures that redefined the skyline and neighborhoods of New York. Recognized for his ability to assemble important sites in key locations throughout Manhattan, my father was a true visionary. His projects were groundbreaking and creative. He could see possibilities in sites that other developers overlooked, and he had an uncanny sense of how changing one pivotal block in a transitional neighborhood could transform the entire area.

I remember my father, a mild-mannered man of few words, sitting at his desk pensively studying the subway map of Manhattan. Pointing out that some of the most important subway locations in Manhattan were rundown, he was evaluating the potential for converting the equally deteriorating neighborhoods serviced by these transportation hubs into new developments. At that time, Broadway and West 96th Street had three subway lines and Union Square had six. I remember his excitement, as his eyes glowed with enthusiasm and exhilaration: could S. Klein department store on Union Square be the gateway for the transformation of downtown Manhattan?

My father was a wonderful person to work with and a thoughtful man to learn from. Personally, he was a strong-willed, determined individual; professionally, he was innovative and futuristic in every respect. Through our dynamic and respectful relationship, I was able to perform multiple roles, which evolved into many successful projects and the creation of landmark buildings throughout New York.

Acknowledged as a pioneer, my father was responsible for creating some of the most complex and challenging real estate developments of the 1980s. In his desire to conquer new frontiers, he took after his great-grandfather, the first William Zeckendorf. A mid-nineteenth-century trader who had emigrated from Germany to the American Southwest, my great-grandfather chose to tackle the difficult and dangerous high-mountain route to trade with Western gold miners and Native American tribes. My father's greatest fulfillment in his career came from tackling difficult, pivotal projects that today stand as iconic buildings on the New York skyline.

My father played an important historical role in transforming and gentrifying Manhattan in the 1980s. The legacy he left is as a catalyst for growth and change, with a clear vision and a strong reverence for architectural detail.

I take great pride in calling William Zeckendorf Jr. my father, and I'm honored to have worked beside him.

Arthur Zeckendorf
New York City, 2016

ACKNOWLEDGMENTS

Like a building, a book is a collective effort. Without publisher Andrea Monfried, who believed that Bill's story deserved a wide audience, *Developing: A Life* would never have made it into print. We also thank designer Yve Ludwig and photo researcher Neil Ryder Hoos.

We are particularly grateful to Gordon Goff, founder and managing director of ORO Editions, and to Kirby Anderson, associate editor, for so capably and graciously publishing the second edition of *Developing*.

Thanks to Fred Dillen, a Santa Fe writer whose many hours of recorded interviews with Bill and others provided essential background. Fred's drafts served as the backbone of the chapters on the Columbia, Worldwide Plaza, and Zeckendorf Towers. Earlier drafts prepared by the late Peter Model also yielded useful material.

While Bill's insight and humor were razor sharp, by his own admission his memory for specifics was not. His trusted lieutenants at the Zeckendorf Company—senior vice presidents and managing directors Tom Javits and Terry Soderberg—were generous in filling in details of the projects they worked on.

Bill was loved and respected by countless friends and colleagues, many of whom were kind enough to supply information and offer observations on Bill as they knew him. We thank the late Herb Sturz, a former chair of the City Planning Commission of New York who partnered with Bill on Citylights in Queens; David Ater and Earl Potter, Bill's partners on several Santa Fe projects; and Daniel Rose, Bill's lifelong friend and member of another noted New York real estate family.

We appreciate input from Skidmore, Owings & Merrill chairman emeritus David Childs, architect of Worldwide Plaza and the Alexandria, and from architect Birch Coffey, who designed interiors for several Zeckendorf projects, as well as Bill and Nancy's apartment in the Hotel Delmonico.

For providing information on Bill's hotel developments, we appreciate the contributions of the late real estate broker Robert Shapiro, the late attorney Neil Underberg, the late hotelier Robert H. Burns, and attorney Peter T. Rado.

We thank Veronica Garaycochea-Williams, wife of the late architect Frank Williams, and Lawrence Adams, a former associate in the Williams office, for relating their memories of Bill and Frank. We also thank Frank's son, David Williams, for permission to reprint his father's sketches and plans. Our thanks to Robert L. Keeney III, president of the Chevaliers du Tastevin Foundation, for additional information on Tastevin.

For her extensive contribution to the chapter on Zeckendorf family history, we are indebted to Bill's cousin Bettina O'Neil Lyons, author of *Zeckendorfs and Steinfelds: Merchant Princes of the American Southwest.*

Special thanks go to Bill's sons, Will and Arthur, who contributed the foreword and afterword, respectively. Their tributes are gracious and loving bookends to their father's words. We also appreciate the photographs and other materials from the Zeckendorf archives.

Finally, we are eternally grateful to Debbie Klein, Nancy's secretary for almost four decades. The unsung heroine and calm center of the project, Debbie kept it humming through thick and thin, helping with everything from coordinating team efforts to rounding up photographs to reading endless revisions.

NZ/JDO

INDEX

Page numbers in *italics* refer to illustrations.

CREDITS

Every effort has been made to contact copyright holders. Please contact the publisher if there are any additions or corrections.

Cover photo: Courtesy Zeckendorf Family.
Back cover: © David Sundberg/Esto. All rights reserved.

Title page
p. 2: William Zeckendorf Jr. Photo: Courtesy Zeckendorf Family.

Introduction
p. 18: WZ Jr. at Zeckendorf Towers construction site. Photo: Michael Singer/Fortune magazine, December 8, 1986.
p. 23: William Zeckendorf Sr. on car phone. Photo: John Loengard/ The LIFE Picture Collection/Getty Images.
p. 24: WZ Jr. with model of Zeckendorf Towers, 1986. Photo: Courtesy Zeckendorf Family.

Growing Up Zeckendorf
p. 30 left: WZ Jr. as a baby, 1929, New York City. Photo: Courtesy Zeckendorf Family.
p. 30 middle: WZ Jr.'s mother, née Irma Levy. Photo: Courtesy Zeckendorf Family.
p. 30 right: WZ Jr. with sister, Susan Zeckendorf. Photo: Courtesy Zeckendorf Family.
p. 31: WZ Jr. at the Lawrenceville School, 1944. Photo: Courtesy Zeckendorf Family.
p. 33: WZ Jr. in US Army, South Korea, 1952. Photo: Courtesy Zeckendorf Family.

Learning the Business
p. 38 left: Rendering of X-City project. *Life* magazine, October 28, 1946.
p. 38 right: United Nations site, New York City. Photo: Charles Payne/NY Daily News/Getty Images.
p. 39: Cartoon by Whitney Darrow Jr., The New Yorker, March 31, 1956. The New Yorker Collection/The Cartoon Bank.
p. 41: WZ Sr. and Her Majesty Queen Elizabeth II view model of Place Ville Marie, Montreal, Quebec, Canada. Photo: Courtesy Place Ville Marie Archives.
p. 43: Century City, Los Angeles, California. Photo: USC Digital Library, Los Angeles Examiner, Photographs Collection.
p. 44: WZ Sr. (center) and US President Dwight D. Eisenhower (left) view rendering of L'Enfant Plaza, Washington, DC, 1955. Photo: Courtesy Zeckendorf Family.
p. 45 left: Kips Bay Plaza under construction. Photo: Everett Collection.
p. 45 right: Site plan, Kips Bay Plaza. Photo: Pei Cobb Fried & Partners.
p. 47: Robie House, Chicago, Illinois, designed by Frank Lloyd Wright. Photo: G.E. Kidder Smith/Corbis Historical/Getty Images.
p. 48: WZ Jr. (left) with WZ Sr., 1964. Photo: Courtesy Zeckendorf Family.
p. 49: WZ Sr. in his office. Photo: The New York World-Telegram & Sun Newspaper Photograph Collection/Library of Congress, Prints and Photographs Division.
p. 53: The Queen Mary Hotel, Long Beach, California. Photo © Queen Mary Archives.
p. 54: London Bridge, Lake Havasu City, Arizona. Photo © Lee W. Nelson.

Moving Up
p. 58 top: Mayfair House. Photo: Aislinn Weidele.
p. 58 bottom: Sheldon S. "Hack" Wilson. Photo: Courtesy Wilson Family.
p. 60: Sirio Maccioni at Le Cirque, 1988. Photo: Gerard Rondeau/Agence VU/Redux.

Saved By a Dog
p. 63: Sarah Korein. Photo: Courtesy Korein Family.
p. 64: Hotel Delmonico. Photo: Bloomberg/ Getty Images.
p. 65: Justin Colin. Photo: Courtesy Zeckendorf Family.
p. 66 top: Regine's, marquee. Photo: Ebet Roberts/Redferns/Getty Images.
p. 66 bottom: Regine's, interior. Photo: Robin Platzer/The Chronicle Collection/Getty Images.

A Nightmare
p. 68: Hotel McAlpin. Photo: FPG/Archive Photos/Getty Images.
p. 70 left: The New Yorker Hotel. Photo: Courtesy The New Yorker/Wyndham Hotels.
p. 70 right: Reverend Sun Myung Moon with followers. Photo: www. tparents.org.

Easy Money
p. 73: The Statler Hilton. Photo: Vintage postcard.

Win Some, Lose Some
p. 75: Barbizon Hotel. Photo: Courtesy NYC Landmarks Preservation Commission.

Opening the Broadway Corridor
p. 80: The Columbia. Sketch by Frank Williams, from *Frank Williams Architect* by Frank Williams. Courtesy David Williams.
p. 81: The Columbia. Photo: Norman McGrath.
p. 83: West 91st Street community garden, Riverside Park. Photo: Courtesy Michael Minn.
p. 85: Frank Williams. Photo: Fred R. Conrad/ The New York Times/Redux.
p. 86: The Princeton. Photo: Norman McGrath.

Looking Up
p. 89: Belvedere Castle, Central Park. Photo: Bo Zaunder/Getty Images.
p. 90 left: The Park Belvedere site plan, from *Frank Williams Architect.* Courtesy David Williams.
p. 90 right: The Park Belvedere under construction. Photo: Courtesy Davis Brody Bond.
p. 91: The Park Belvedere. Photo: Courtesy Davis Brody Bond.

Win-Win with the A&P
p. 94: The Copley. Photo: Courtesy Davis Brody Bond.
p. 95: The Copley. Photo: Norman McGrath.

Location, Location
p. 98: New York Coliseum. Photo: Vintage postcard.
p. 99: Central Park Place. Photo: Courtesy Davis Brody Bond.
p. 100: Central Park Place, East facade. Photo: Courtesy Davis Brody Bond.
p. 103: 4 Columbus Circle, Central Park Place annex. Photo: Aislinn Weidele.

At a Crossroads
p. 107 left: The Alexandria. Photo: Jeff Goldberg/ Esto. All rights reserved.
p. 107 right: The Alexandria. Sketch by Frank Williams, from *Frank Williams Architect.* Courtesy David Williams.

A Noble Experiment
p. 112: Rendering of Delmonico Plaza. Courtesy Davis Brody Bond.
p. 113: Delmonico Plaza. Photo: Norman McGrath.

Selling Convenience
p. 116 left: The Cosmopolitan. Photo: Norman McGrath.
p. 116 right: The Vanderbilt. Photo: Jeff Goldberg/Esto. All rights reserved.

Breaking New Ground
p. 119: The Belaire. Rendering by Michael McCann. From *The Architecture of Frank Williams* by Michael J. Crosbie. Courtesy David Williams.
p. 120: Tom Javits. Photo: Courtesy Tom Javits.
p. 121: The Belaire. Sketch by Frank Williams, from *Frank Williams Architect.* Courtesy David Williams.
p. 122: The Belaire. Photo: Jeff Goldberg/Esto. All rights reserved.
p. 124 left: Park Avenue Court. Photo: Courtesy CityRealty.
p. 124 right: The Gotham. Photo: Jeff Goldberg/ Esto. All rights reserved.

Downtown

p. 127 left: Hudson Tower, Battery Park City. Photo: Courtesy Davis Brody Bond.

p. 127 right: Site plan of Battery Park City. Courtesy batteryparkcity.org.

Revitalizing Union Square

p. 132: WZ Jr. and sons Will (left) and Arthur with Zeckendorf Towers model. Photo: Fred R. Conrad/The New York Times/Redux.

p. 133: Zeckendorf Towers. Photo: © Nathaniel Lieberman.

p. 134: View of S. Klein at Union Square, 1930. Photo: Percy Loomis Sperr © Milstein Division, The New York Public Library.

p. 136: Sam Brody (left) and Lew Davis with photo of Zeckendorf Towers. Photo: Frank Schramm/Courtesy Davis Brody Bond.

p. 139: WZ Jr. and sons Arthur (left) and Will. Photo: © Alice Garik.

p. 140: Zeckendorf Towers at night. Photo: NewYorkDailyPhoto.com/Brian Dubé.

Opening Up Eighth Avenue

p. 143: Circus comes to old Madison Square Garden. Photo: Jacob Harris/AP Images.

p. 146: Worldwide Plaza. Photo: Jeff Goldberg/ Esto. All rights reserved.

p. 148: David Childs. Photo: © Greg Betz/ Courtesy Skidmore, Owings & Merrill.

p. 150: Worldwide Plaza. Illustration: Courtesy The Zeckendorf Group.

p. 153: WZ Jr. and Mayor Ed Koch with Worldwide Plaza model. Photo: Mario Cabrera/AP Images.

p. 156: Worldwide Plaza entrance. Photo: Jeff Goldberg/Esto. All rights reserved.

p. 157: Worldwide Plaza arcade. Photo: David Sundberg/Esto. All rights reserved.

p. 159: Worldwide Plaza cupola. Photo: © Antony Wood/CTBUH.

p. 160: Worldwide Plaza at night. Photo: © David Sundberg/Esto. All rights reserved.

A Capitol First

p. 163: Federal Triangle, Washington DC (aerial view). Photo: Courtesy Pei Cobb Freed & Partners.

p. 164 top: James Ingo Freed. Photo: Courtesy United States Holocaust Memorial Museum.

p. 164 bottom: Terry Soderberg. Photo: Tom Allen/The Washington Post/Getty Images.

p. 166: Rendering of Ronald Reagan Building. Photo: Courtesy Pei Cobb Freed & Partners.

p. 167: Reagan Building, aerial view. Photo: Courtesy Pei Cobb Freed & Partners.

p. 168: Reagan Building. Photo: © Tim Hursley.

p. 169: Reagan Building atrium. Photo: © Tim Hursley.

p. 171: Reagan Building dedication ceremony. Photo: Courtesy William B. Willis/FTPM Partnership.

Turnaround in Queens

p. 174: WZ Sr. with United Nations in background. Photo: John Loengard/The LIFE Picture Collection/Getty Images.

p. 175 top: Cesar Pelli. Photo: Peter Freed, Architectural Digest © Condé Nast.

p. 175 bottom: Herb Sturz. Photo: Maggie Soladay/Courtesy Open Society Foundations.

p. 176: Pepsi-Cola sign, Long Island City, New York. Photo: Sherab/Alamy.

p. 177: Citylights, Long Island City. Photo: Nate Lindsey/Emporis.

p. 178: Citylights model. Photo: Courtesy Pelli Clarke Pelli Architects.

p. 179: Citylights brochure cover art. Courtesy Rick Meyerowitz.

Lighting Up Times Square

p. 185: The Pussycat Theater. Photo: Courtesy Artkraft Strauss Archive.

p. 186: Rendering of Crowne Plaza Hotel. From *The Architecture of Frank Williams*. Courtesy David Williams.

p. 188: Alan Lapidus. Photo: Courtesy Alexei Tylevich.

p. 189: Crowne Plaza Hotel, Broadway facade. Photo: Peter Mauss/Esto. All rights reserved.

p. 190: Crowne Plaza Hotel, office base with signs. Photo: Paul Bartholomew.

A Royal Mess

p. 195: The Rihga Royal Hotel. Photo credit: Tectonic/Emporis.

p. 196: Model of the Rihga Royal Hotel. Photo: Jeff Goldberg/Esto. All rights reserved.

p. 197: Birch Coffey. Photo: Courtesy Birch Coffey.

p. 198 left: The Rihga Royal Hotel, dining room. Photo: Courtesy Birch Coffey.

p. 198 right: The Rihga Royal Hotel, private dining room. Photo: Courtesy Birch Coffey.

A Crowning Achievement

p. 200: WZ Jr. and I.M. Pei with model of the Four Seasons Hotel. Photo: Courtesy Zeckendorf Family.

p. 207: WZ Jr. with son Will (left) and an associate in Japan. Photo: Courtesy Zeckendorf Family.

p. 208: WZ Jr. (center) and architects Frank Williams (2nd from right) and I.M. Pei (far right) with investors and model of the Four Seasons Hotel. Photo: Courtesy Zeckendorf Family.

p. 209: The Four Seasons Hotel. Sketch by Frank Williams, from *Frank Williams Architect*. Courtesy David Williams.

p. 210: The Four Seasons Hotel. Photo: Jeff Goldberg/Esto. All rights reserved.

p. 211: WZ Jr., Nancy Zeckendorf, and I.M. Pei at the Louvre. Photo: Courtesy Zeckendorf Family.

p. 213: The Four Seasons Hotel entrance. Photo: © Eric Nathan/Alamy Stock Photo.

515 Park

p. 218: 515 Park Avenue. Photo: Jeff Goldberg/ Esto. All rights reserved.

p. 224: WZ Jr. with sons Will (left) and Arthur, and associates at 515 Park construction site. Photo: Steve Friedman.

Leaving New York

p. 229: Zeckendorf house in Chappaqua, New York. Photo: Courtesy Zeckendorf Family.

The Zeckendorfs in the Southwest

p. 234: William Zeckendorf in Tucson, Arizona, 1875. Archival photo: Arizona Historical Society.

p. 235: WZ Jr. and WZ Sr. at replica of general store. Photo: Courtesy Zeckendorf Family.

p. 237: William Zeckendorf and wife, née Julia Frank, c. 1900. Photo: Courtesy Bettina O'Neill Lyons.

p. 238: Zeckendorf & Staab, Tucson, Arizona. Archival photo: Stereo collection, Arizona Historical Society.

p. 239: Wm. Zeckendorf store advertisement, September 25, 1880. Photo: Reprinted with permission from the Arizona Daily Star.

Nancy Zeckendorf

p. 241 left: Nancy Zeckendorf (née King) in *Carmen*. Photo: Daniel Entin. Courtesy Zeckendorf Family.

p. 241 right: Nancy Zeckendorf (née King) in *Don Quixote*. Photo: Rad Bascome. Courtesy Zeckendorf Family.

p. 242 left: Nancy and WZ Jr. wedding photo. Photo: Bradford Bachrach/Courtesy Zeckendorf Family.

p. 242 right: WZ Jr. and Nancy at Taj Mahal, India. Photo: Courtesy Zeckendorf Family.

p. 243 left: Second Santa Fe opera house, built 1967. Photo: Alex Irvin. Courtesy Santa Fe Performing Arts Center.

p. 243 right: Nancy Zeckendorf and John Crosby. Photo: Courtesy Zeckendorf Family.

p. 244 top: New Santa Fe opera house. Photo: Goodwin/Courtesy of Santa Fe Performing Arts Center.

p. 244 bottom: Santa Fe opera house interior. Photo: Robert Reck.

Scenic Views

p. 246: Los Miradores. Photo of oil painting. Used with permission.

p. 247: Los Miradores. Photo from sales brochure. Used with permission.

p. 249 top: Nancy Zeckendorf. Photo: Courtesy Zeckendorf Family.

p. 249 bottom: WZ Jr. and Nancy at home at Los Miradores. Photo: Courtesy Zeckendorf Family.

Successful Sight Planning

p. 252 left: Zeckendorf house at Sierra del Norte, exterior. Photo: Peter Vitale.
p. 252 right: Sierra del Norte house, living room. Photo: Peter Vitale.
p. 253 left: Sierra del Norte house, wine room. Photo: Peter Vitale.
p. 253 right: WZ Sr.'s desk in Sierra del Norte music room. Photo: Peter Vitale.

Introducing Luxury

p. 256: Nancy Zeckendorf at Big Jo Lumber, Santa Fe. Photo: © 1983 Linda Montoya/ Courtesy Zeckendorf Family.
p. 258: The El Dorado Hotel, Santa Fe. Photo: Courtesy eldoradohotel.com.
p. 260: The Hotel Santa Fe, front. Photo: Courtesy Hotel Santa Fe.
p. 261: The Hotel Santa Fe, patio. Photo: Courtesy Hotel Santa Fe.

Restoring A Landmark

p. 265: Painting of the Lensic theater by Odon Hullenkremer. Photo: Courtesy Zeckendorf Family.
p. 268 top and bottom: The Lensic under renovation. Photos: Grant Taylor/Courtesy Lensic Performing Arts Center.
p. 270 left: The Lensic restored, exterior. Photo: Robert Reck/Courtesy Lensic Performing Arts Center.
p. 270 right: The Lensic stage. Photo: Robert Reck/Courtesy Lensic Performing Arts Center.

An Inherited Taste

p. 274: WZ Jr.'s induction into Tastevin, 1958. Photo: Courtesy Zeckendorf Family.
p. 275: WZ Jr. and son Will. Photo: Courtesy Zeckendorf Family.
p. 276: WZ Jr. receiving Tastevin honor from Kelly Shannon. Photo: Courtesy Zeckendorf Family.

Giving Back

p. 278: WZ Jr., David Steinberg, and Derek Bok. Photo: Courtesy Long Island University.
p. 280: William Zeckendorf Health Sciences Center, Long Island University, Brooklyn, New York. Photo: Jeff Goldberg/Esto. All rights reserved.

Three Generations

p. 282: Will (left) and Arthur Zeckendorf as children. Photo: Courtesy Zeckendorf Family.
p. 283: WZ Jr. with sons Will (left) and Arthur. Photo: Steve Friedman.
p. 284 left: 15 Central Park West. Photo: © Peter Aaron/ OTTO for Robert A.M. Stern Architects.
p. 284 right: Will (left) and Arthur Zeckendorf at 50 United Nations Plaza. Photo: Mary Altaffer/AP Images.
p. 285 left: WZ Sr., WZ Jr., and Will Zeckendorf. Photo: Courtesy Zeckendorf Family.
p. 285 middle: WZ Jr. and grandson Arthur Zeckendorf Jr. Photo: Courtesy Zeckendorf Family.
p. 285 right: Granddaughter Jennifer Zeckendorf. Photo: Courtesy Zeckendorf Family.

Summing Up

p. 288: WZ Jr. with (from left) Arthur, Will, and Nancy Zeckendorf; Eileen Pei, Frank Williams, and I.M. Pei. Photo: Courtesy Zeckendorf Family.

Epilogue

p. 290: WZ Jr. Photo: Courtesy Zeckendorf Family.

6
23
22
1
7
4
15
19
10
14
11
12
24
27
9
8
25
20
26
28
16
18
17